GALLUP
YOUTH
SURVEY:

MAJOR ISSUES AND TRENDS

TEENS &
CHEATING

Hal Marcovitz

**Developed in
Association with the
Gallup Organization**

Teens & Alcohol

Teens & Career Choices

Teens & Cheating

Teens & Family Issues

Teens, Health, & Obesity

Teens & LGBT Issues

Teens & the Media

Teens & Race

Teens & Relationships

Teens, Religion, & Values

Teens & Sex

Teens & Suicide

Teens & the Supernatural/Paranormal

Teens & Volunteerism

GALLUP
YOUTH
SURVEY:

MAJOR ISSUES AND TRENDS

TEENS &
CHEATING

Hal Marcovitz

**Developed in
Association with the
Gallup Organization**

Mason Crest
450 Parkway Drive, Suite D
Broomall, PA 19008
www.masoncrest.com

Printed and bound in the United States of America.

CPSIA Compliance Information: Batch #GYS2013. For further information, contact Mason Crest at 1-866-MCP-Book

First printing
1 3 5 7 9 8 6 4 2

Library of Congress Cataloging-in-Publication Data

Marcovitz, Hal.
  Teens and cheating / Hal Marcovitz.
      pages cm. — (The Gallup youth survey : major issues and trends)
  Includes bibliographical references and index.
  Audience: Grade 7 to 8.
  ISBN 978-1-4222-2951-4 (hc)
  ISBN 978-1-4222-8868-9 (ebook)
  1. Children—Conduct of life—Juvenile literature. 2. Cheating—Juvenile literature. I. Title.
  BJ1631.M33 2014
  179'.8—dc23
                                  2013007240

The Gallup Youth Survey: Major Issues and Trends series ISBN: 978-1-4222-2948-4

Contents

As the United States moves into the new century, there is a vital need for insight into what it means to be a young person in America. Today's teenagers will be the leaders and shapers of the 21st century. The future direction of the United States is being determined now in their hearts and minds and actions. Yet how much do we as a society know about this important segment of the U.S. populace who have the potential to lift our nation to new levels of achievement and social health?

We need to hear the voices of young people, and to help them better articulate their fears and their hopes. Our youth have much to share with their elders—is the older generation really listening? Is it carefully monitoring the hopes and fears of teenagers today? Failure to do so could result in severe social consequences.

The Gallup Youth Survey was conducted between 1977 and 2006 to help society meet this responsibility to youth, as well as to inform and guide our leaders by probing the social and economic attitudes and behaviors of young people. With theories abounding about the views, lifestyles, and values of adolescents, the Gallup Youth Survey, through regular scientific measurements of teens themselves, served as a sort of reality check.

Surveys reveal that the image of teens in the United States today is a negative one. Teens are frequently maligned, misunderstood, or simply ignored by their elders. Yet over four decades the Gallup Youth Survey provided ample evidence of the very special qualities of the nation's youngsters. In fact, if our society is less racist, less sexist, less polluted, and more peace loving, we can in considerable measure thank our young people, who have been on the leading edge on these issues. And the younger generation is not geared to greed: survey after survey has shown that teens have a keen interest in helping those people, especially in their own communities, who are less fortunate than themselves

Young people have told Gallup that they are enthusiastic about helping others, and are willing to work for world peace and a healthy world. They feel positive about their schools and even more positive about their teachers. A large majority of American teenagers have reported that they are happy and excited about the future, feel very close to their families, are likely to marry, want to have children, are satisfied with their personal lives, and desire to reach the top of their chosen careers.

But young adults face many threats, so parents, guardians, and concerned adults must commit themselves to do everything possible to help tomorrow's parents, citizens, and leaders avoid or overcome risky behaviors so that they can move into the future with greater hope and understanding.

The Gallup Organization is enthusiastic about this partnership with Mason Crest Publishers. Through carefully and clearly written books on a variety of vital topics dealing with teens, Gallup Youth Survey statistics are presented in a way that gives new depth and meaning to the data. The focus of these books is a practical one—to provide readers with the statistics and solid information that they need to understand and to deal with each important topic.

— — —

"Cheating has turned into a national epidemic among young people," writes the author of this book. Surveys and other data support this statement, and point to a situation that appears to be growing steadily worse. Teens appear to be taking their cue from the larger society, which seems increasingly less likely to value truth-telling and offers fewer role models in this respect. Cheating is pervasive, infecting the academic, professional, and financial worlds, as well as other areas of life.

The author notes that family, church, and schools have been unable to stop the trend of cheating. New and creative approaches and programs need to be put forth, examples of which are offered in this book. Failure to stem this tide will result in youngsters today bringing any proclivities to cheat into future roles of leadership and responsibility in their communities and in the nation.

Chapter One

Many observers believe cheating has become a major problem in schools today. Surveys have shown that between 50 and 75 percent of students admit to having cheated on a test or exam at least once.

A National Epidemic of Cheating

Jonathan Lebed seemed like the typical teenager. Tall and lanky, the 15-year-old high school sophomore from Cedar Grove, New Jersey, favored baggy jeans, a spiked haircut, sneakers, and a piercing in his ear. He liked the New York Mets and loved pro wrestling so much that he developed a World Wide Web site dedicated to his favorite wrestler, Stone Cold Steve Austin.

Jonathan did more on the Internet than follow Steve Austin's career, though. In 1996, when Jonathan turned 12 years old, a United States savings bond that his parents bought for him matured, meaning it could be cashed in. The bond paid $8,000. Instead of putting the money into the bank to save for college or another important reason, Jonathan had other ideas. He talked his parents into letting him invest the money in the stock market.

Millions of Americans own shares of stock, which means they own a stake in a business or businesses. To raise money to develop and manufacture new products, companies often make shares of their stock available for sale to the public. The shares are actually pieces of the company; therefore, the owner of the shares (a stockholder) is an owner of a percentage of the company. Shares of stock are traded on markets called exchanges, where brokers buy and sell shares for their clients, the investors. If a company is profitable and its prospects look good, the shares often rise in value—sometimes substantially in the course of a single day. On the other hand, if a company's prospects are dim, the value of the stock may fall. It is not unusual for a company's stock to lose considerable value in a single day.

Many investors buy and sell stocks on the Internet and have established accounts in Internet-based brokerage firms. With a few simple keystrokes an investor can place an order to buy or sell stocks. If the investor sells a stock at a higher price than he or she paid for it, a profit can be made.

Jonathan Lebed proved to be very good at finding stocks that would rise in value. In fact, he took that first $8,000 and invested it entirely in America Online, the Internet service provider, buying 320 shares at $25 each. After a few weeks, the value of America Online rose to $30 a share. Jonathan sold it, making a profit of $1,600 before brokerage fees and taxes. It was easy money. Jonathan Lebed was hooked.

Soon, he was trading thousands of shares of stock through his Internet account and making tens of thousands of dollars. He would rise at 5 A.M. each day so he could spend time before school watching investment experts talk about stocks on CNBC, the cable TV network devoted to news about the stock market. He learned that the value of a stock would often rise when an analyst appearing on CNBC would talk about the stock, hyping it for investors. It seemed to Jonathan that people who bought and sold stocks often did so simply because somebody on CNBC said it was a good idea. He suspected that very few investors bother to do their own research on a company, exploring its prospects for the future as well as its past performance. It did not even seem to matter whether a company was making or losing money. Most people, he concluded, invested only to make a quick profit.

"People who trade stocks, trade based on what they feel will move and they can trade for profit," Jonathan explained in an e-mail that was later quoted in a news article by the *New York Times*. "Nobody makes investment decisions based on reading financial filings. Whether a company is making millions or losing millions, it has no impact on the price of a stock. Whether it is analysts, brokers, advisors, Internet traders or the companies, everybody is manipulating the market."

Jonathan Lebed decided to see if people would respond to hype about stocks he owned. So he created a series of phony identities, visited an Internet chat room devoted to the stock market, and started writing messages to the chat room visitors talking about stocks he owned—always anonymously and always in glowing terms. For example, in reference to one stock he wrote, "Next week, this thing will EXPLODE . . ." Another message said, "I am hearing that a number of HUGE deals are being worked on . . . Once we get some news . . . and the word gets out about the company . . . it will take off to MUCH HIGHER LEVELS."

"In the beginning, I would write, like, very professionally," Jonathan explained in an interview with the *New York Times*. "But then I started putting stuff in caps and using exclamation points and making it sound more exciting. That worked better. When it's more exciting, it draws people's attention to it compared to when you write, like, dull or something."

The development of the Internet made it possible for young people like Jonathan Lebed to easily trade stocks from home. Lebed cheated the markets by making up stock tips for people seeking investment advice on the Internet, therefore increasing the value of his own holdings.

Investors did pay attention, and some started buying the stocks. When demand is created for a stock, the price rises. Over the course of several months, Jonathan hyped 11 stocks that way, and each time the price shot up dramatically. He always sold his shares when the price reached a very high level. By the time the government caught up with him, Jonathan had cleared a profit of some $800,000.

Of course, what Jonathan Lebed was engaged in was cheating. When the Securities and Exchange Commission, the government agency in charge of making sure stocks are sold in a fair market, found out what Jonathan was up to, it stopped his trading and made Jonathan pay back a large share of the money. "I find his case very disturbing . . . more serious than the guy who holds up the candy store," Securities and Exchange Commission Chairman Arthur Levitt told the *New York Times*. "Put it this way: he'd buy, lie, and sell high."

Cheating More Than Ever

The case of Jonathan Lebed is unique. The Securities and Exchange Commission said he was the first adolescent ever investigated for illegally manipulating the value of stocks. Not many teenagers know how to trade stocks, let alone figure out ways to cheat their way to high profits. By no means, however, is Jonathan the first teenager who has ever been caught cheating.

Cheating has turned into a national epidemic among young people. Studies show that more teenagers are cheating than ever before. They cheat in school, they cheat in sports, and they cheat at home. The Gallup Organization, a national polling firm, has often studied how teens view cheating through the Gallup Youth Survey, a longtime project by the firm to assess the ideas of young people in the United States. In 1984, the Gallup Youth Survey determined that 94 percent of the teens who responded to a poll said they regard the trait of honesty as "very important." Two decades later, the Gallup Youth Survey found far different results. In 2001, a poll conducted among 454 young people between the ages of 13 and 17 found that just 43 percent of the respondents said they regard honesty as a trait found in a person of "good character."

Why do more than half of the teens surveyed believe that somebody of good character does not necessarily have to be honest? Perhaps because many of the teenagers who responded to the survey admitted to cheating and telling lies themselves. A total of

TEEN MORALITY

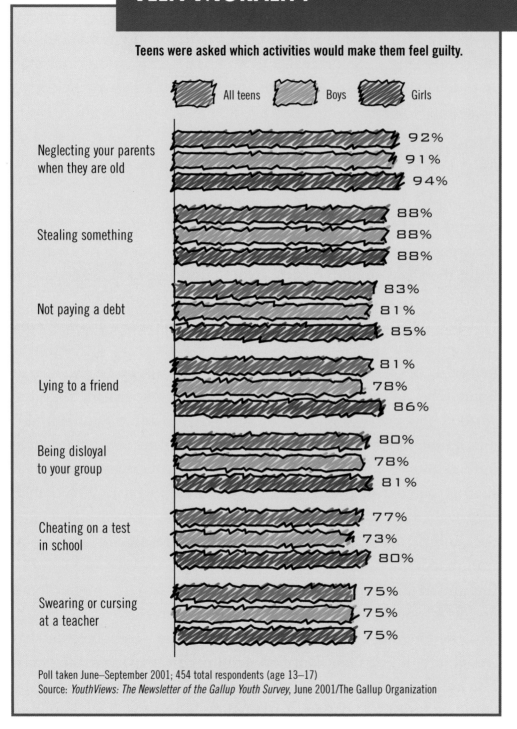

Teens were asked which activities would make them feel guilty.

All teens   Boys   Girls

Neglecting your parents when they are old
- 92%
- 91%
- 94%

Stealing something
- 88%
- 88%
- 88%

Not paying a debt
- 83%
- 81%
- 85%

Lying to a friend
- 81%
- 78%
- 86%

Being disloyal to your group
- 80%
- 78%
- 81%

Cheating on a test in school
- 77%
- 73%
- 80%

Swearing or cursing at a teacher
- 75%
- 75%
- 75%

Poll taken June–September 2001; 454 total respondents (age 13–17)
Source: *YouthViews: The Newsletter of the Gallup Youth Survey*, June 2001/The Gallup Organization

73 percent of the respondents agreed with the statement "I sometimes tell lies if I have to." Also, 44 percent of the respondents admitted to cheating on tests. The Gallup Youth Survey found that older teens cheat more than younger teens: 37 percent of young people between the ages of 13 and 15 admitted to cheating, while that number grew to 53 percent for 16- and 17-year-old students. Parents and teachers could take some comfort in the fact that 77 percent of the respondents admitted that when they cheat, they feel guilty about it. Of course, that also means that nearly a quarter of all teenagers *do not* feel guilty about cheating.

This book will explore the reasons teenagers cheat and it will look at where they cheat. Not surprisingly, many teenagers confine their cheating to school, where they are under considerable pressure to make good grades so they can be accepted into top colleges. But teenagers cheat in other places. In sports, for example, it is becoming common to find teenage athletes taking steroids and other illegal performance-enhancing drugs. At home, teenagers readily download music over the Internet—an act that violates copyright laws and cheats the recording company as well as the artist out of royalties. Finally, this book will examine teenagers and ethics and where they learn particular ethical lesson, including at home, at church, and in school. Teenagers also often develop an honor code of their own with a skewed set of values that adults may have a hard time understanding.

Cheating Is Everywhere

Experts believe that young people cheat for the same reasons that adults cheat: they want something that they lack the skills, knowledge, talent, money, or patience to achieve. To get a good grade on a test in a class that is giving her trouble, a student may steal a glance at a friend's test. A good grade on the test may be the difference between passing and failing the class, which may have a lot to do with the type of college that would accept the student. The student may have studied, or maybe not. For whatever reason, she finds herself in class that day unprepared to take the test. So she cheats.

"Cheating is everywhere," wrote author David Callahan in his book *The Cheating Culture*. "By cheating, I mean breaking the rules to get ahead academically, professionally, or financially. Some of this cheating involves violating the law; some does not. Either way, most of it is by people who, on the whole, view themselves as upstanding members of society. Again and again, Americans who wouldn't so much as shoplift a pack of chewing gum are committing felonies at tax time, betraying the trust of their parents, misleading investors, ripping off their insurance company, or lying to their clients."

In his book, Callahan points out that it is very difficult to measure the amount of cheating that is going on. After all, cheating is usually done in secret and good cheaters get away with cheating because nobody finds out. Cases such as Jonathan Lebed's are rare—he left a paper and electronic trail of his activities that the Securities and Exchange Commission was easily able to follow. But unless the student stealing a glance at her friend's test is caught by the teacher, chances are the cheating will go undetected.

Still, some groups do try to gauge trends in cheating. One such organization is the California-based Joseph and Edna Josephson Institute Center for Youth Ethics. Every two years, the institute conducts a survey on cheating by young people. The 2012 survey polled 23,000 high school students on the subject. The survey found that 51 percent of the respondents admitted to cheating at least once on a test in the 12 months preceding the survey. Fifty-five percent said they had lied to a teacher in the past year about something significant. Thirty-two percent said they had copied an Internet document for a classroom assignment and passed it off as their own work. Twenty percent said they had stolen something from a store in the past year.

Among the other findings of the Josephson report was that boys are more likely to harbor negative attitudes and engage in dishonest conduct than girls. The 2012 survey found that 45 percent of boys believed that "a person has to lie and cheat at least occasionally in order to succeed," compared to 28 percent of girls

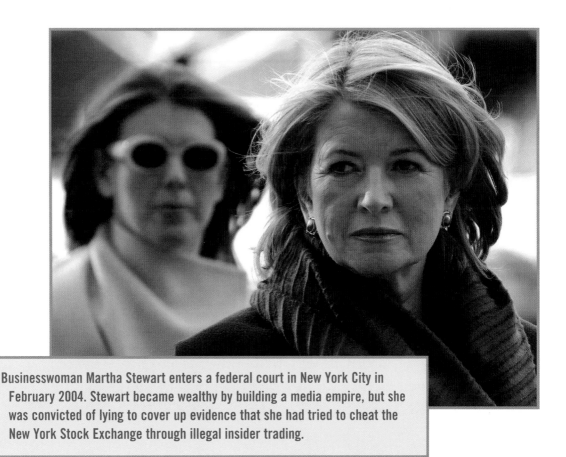

Businesswoman Martha Stewart enters a federal court in New York City in February 2004. Stewart became wealthy by building a media empire, but she was convicted of lying to cover up evidence that she had tried to cheat the New York Stock Exchange through illegal insider trading.

who believe this. Boys were almost twice as likely to steal from a friend as girls (19 percent compared to 10 percent).

The Josephson Institute found that cheating is widespread despite the efforts of parents, teachers, and other authority figures. According to the 2012 report, 93 percent of students said their parents or guardians always wanted them to do the ethically right thing, no matter the cost. Eighty-five percent said that most adults in their lives consistently set a good example in terms of ethics and character.

Changing Values

Another organization that has followed trends in cheating is Educational Communications Inc., publisher of *Who's Who Among American High School Students*. In 1999, the publisher polled high-achieving students on their attitudes about a number of subjects. A total of 84 percent said cheating is "common" among their peers, while 78 percent of the students—all high achievers, remember—admitted to cheating themselves. (Ninety-five percent of them said they had not been caught.) The *Who's Who* survey asked the students to talk about their motivations for cheating. A total of 56 percent said they cheated to achieve good grades; 56 percent said they cheated because they thought cheating was no big deal; 30 percent said they cheated because they had no interest in what they were studying; 25 percent said they cheated because they did not think they would get caught; and 16 percent said they cheated to get into a good college.

Those answers tell a lot about why young people cheat. Clearly, many of them believe they are under pressure to do well and are prepared to do whatever it takes to achieve their goals. And some of them have convinced themselves they face no moral dilemmas in making the choice to cheat—just look at how many high-achieving students said they cheated because it was no big deal. "You have to understand how the values of American society have changed over the past quarter of a century. Simply put, we have a nastier, more cutthroat set of values than previous generations did," writes David Callahan in *The Cheating Culture*. "As the race for money and status has intensified, it has become more acceptable for individuals to act more opportunistically and dishonestly to get ahead. Notions of integrity have weakened. More of us are willing to make the wrong choices, at least when it comes to money and career."

Despite what some parents may think, teenagers do not live entirely in their own world. They are aware of what is going on around them and they do pay attention to how adults act. And what they see in the adult world is a lot of cheating. In 2012, bike racer Lance Armstrong made national headlines when he admitted to taking banned substances in order to win the Tour de France, cycling's most prestigious race, seven times. Since the late 1990s, the news media has reported on scandals involving executives from such corporations as Enron, Arthur Andersen, and WorldCom who were found to have cheated employees, customers, and stockholders of millions of dollars. In 2010, the Securities and Exchange Commission charged the powerful investment banking firm Goldman Sachs with defrauding investor in order to make a $1 billion profit. And after the 2012 presidential election, young people probably heard accusations that political leaders had blocked access to polling places by African-American and Latino voters, or, on the other extreme, had illegally bused minority voters into polling places, thereby attempting to swing the election to a particular candidate.

Many Americans considered Lance Armstrong an inspirational hero, because he successfully overcame cancer to win the Tour de France a record seven straight times between 1999 and 2005. However, in 2012 the United States Anti-Doping Agency (USADA) claimed that he had used prohibitied drugs to win the races. His victories were vacated and he was banned from cycling for life.

Subsequent investigations found no evidence of voter fraud, yet many Americans chose to believe it had occurred.

Is it any wonder, then, that young people look at how adults act and conclude that cheating is no big deal? Clearly, they have reached the decision that cheating is OK because as far as they can tell, everybody does it. What has become painfully clear is that the stories told by Horatio Alger Jr. are no longer the norm in American society. Alger was a 19th-century author who wrote stories about young boys from humble circumstances who were able to achieve wealth and fame through honest hard work. The hero in a Horatio Alger story would never think of cheating to get ahead.

Alice Newhall, a 17-year-old student at George Mason High School in Virginia, was asked by a reporter for CNN why she thinks her classmates cheat. "What's important is getting ahead," she answered. "The better grades you have, the better school you get into, the better you're going to do in life. And if you learn to cut corners to do that, you're going to be saving yourself time and energy. In the real world, that's what's going to be going on. The better you do, that's what shows. It's not how moral you were in getting there."

What is lost in that explanation, though, is recognition that somebody always gets hurt by cheaters. Is it fair to the student who stayed home to study to properly prepare for the test to have his or her answers stolen? How does the recording artist feel about losing royalties to unpaid Internet downloads? What about the athlete who loses a major-league job because he has been replaced by a player who is taking drugs that enhance his performance? "Widespread cheating is undermining some of the most important ideals of American society," writes David Callahan. "The principal of equal opportunity is subverted when those who play by the rules are beaten out by cheaters, as happens every day in academics, sports, business, and other arenas. The belief that hard work is the key to success is mocked when people see, constantly, that success comes faster to those who cut corners."

Chapter Two

A boy glances at his friend's paper during a test. Pressure on young people to get good grades and be accepted into a top college sometimes causes even the brightest students to feel they must cheat to stay ahead.

Succumbing to Temptation

The students at Harvard University, one of America's most prestigious colleges, are expected to be high achievers. They are expected to take honors courses and maintain high grade-point averages, and win admission to competitive colleges. In 2012, however, approximately 125 Harvard students were caught cheating on an examination for a course in government.

The professor who taught the Harvard course Government 1310: "Introduction to Congress" determined students' grades using four take-home exams. When assistants were grading the exams in May 2012, they noticed that many of them shared similar language. The university launched an investigation, and soon learned that many students had worked on the exam in small groups, even though the instructions for the take-home test said that they had to work alone.

Ultimately, more than 75 Harvard students were suspended from the university, and about 25 others received disciplinary probation. In a statement released by the university, Harvard president Drew Gilpin Faust said, "These allegations, if proven, represent totally unacceptable behavior that betrays the trust upon which intellectual inquiry at Harvard depends. . . . The scope of the allegations suggests that there is work to be done to ensure that every student at Harvard understands and embraces the values that are fundamental to its community of scholars."

The SAT and Perfect Scores

Cheating has become such a way of life among students that in 2004 a Hollywood studio released *The Perfect Score*, a film dramatizing the adventures of six students who plot to break into the

A scene from the 2004 film *The Perfect Score*, in which a group of teenagers conspire to steal the answers to the Scholastic Aptitude Test (SAT).

Princeton, New Jersey, headquarters of Educational Testing Service (ETS), the organization that administers the SAT. The prime motivation of the burglars is to attain high SAT scores so they can win admissions to top colleges. Kyle, one of the characters in the film, has his sights set on Cornell University, where he plans to study architecture, but knows he cannot win admission with his dismal SAT scores. Instead of electing to study hard and take the test again, Kyle plans the break-in. During the film, Kyle justifies the plot to a friend. He says, "Don't you find it ridiculous that from Day One they tell us to be unique, they tell us to be individuals, then they give us a standardized test that makes us all one faceless herd?"

The irony of *The Perfect Score* is that even if Kyle and his friends could pull off the burglary and swipe the answers, it is likely they would have been singled out as cheaters, anyway. Educational Testing Service routinely questions the test results of any student who takes the SAT a second time and attains a score 350 points higher than his initial score. Taking the test a second time typically adds just 50 or 100 points to a score, so the organization is on the lookout for dramatic jumps in students' scores. "If you have a combined increase [of 350 points] it will at least cause us to take a look. It is very, if not extremely, unusual," Educational Testing Service spokesman Tom Ewing told the *Newark Star-Ledger*.

How rare is a bona fide perfect score on the SAT? In 2012, some 1.66 million college-bound students took the SAT. Of all those test takers, just 360 achieved a perfect score of 2400. And even in the unlikely event that somebody could steal and memorize the test answers, score a 2400, and manage to fool Educational Testing Service, a perfect SAT does not guarantee automatic admission to the nation's top schools. True, college entrance examination scores do count a lot, but highly competitive schools look for a lot more in a student, such as a high grade-point average, leadership and a record of service in school and the community, a well-written essay, and a background that would add to the diversity of the student body.

Still, cheating on the SAT is not as outlandish as it may sound. Any student who has taken the lengthy and rigorous examination knows the drill all too well: the student shows up on test day and is sent to a classroom. Arriving at the classroom, the student finds the seats are assigned. The seats are placed three feet apart to discourage students from stealing peeks at their neighbors' tests. A proctor remains in the room for the entire three hours of the test and must follow a 59-page rulebook for administering the examination. Cell phones are prohibited in the testing center to make sure the students cannot call or text message friends for answers or access the Internet for help. Calculators are permitted, but not hand-held electronic dictionaries. To enter the classroom, a student has to show photo identification. With all that security, how can anyone get away with cheating on the SAT? Plenty of students try, but few succeed.

Conspirators to Cheating

For the SAT, students are encouraged to bring snacks into the testing center with them. An innocent practice, to be sure: students get hungry, which can distract them from the task of taking the test. But even food can be used to cheat. Proctors have caught students arranging different colored M&M candies on their desks in order to signal test answers to their friends. "We do all we can to make sure the test is secure," Educational Testing Service spokeswoman Kristen Carnahan told the *Atlanta Journal Constitution.*

"Are there instances of cheating that are looked into? I have no information on trends about that. We just do the best we can. There's no clear trend of it getting worse."

Still, there is no getting around the fact that cheating does occur. According to Educational Testing Service, about 3,000 scores are canceled each year because of suspected cheating. About 150 of these each year are cases in which a person takes the test while pretending to be another student, so that the student gets credit for a score he or she did not actually earn. In November 2011, for example, authorities arrested five young men who had conducted a test-taking service in the affluent community of Great Neck, Long Island. For a fee of around $3,600, the five created false IDs and took the SAT or ACT, another college entrance exam, on behalf of the students who had hired them. The five were charged with fraud, criminal impersonation, and falsifying business records, while 15 high school students who had paid for their services were also arrested and charged with misdemeanors.

Two other standardized tests that are similar to the SAT are the Graduate Record Examination (GRE) and the Graduate Management Admission Test (GMAT), both of which are taken by college students who seek admission to graduate schools. Like the SAT, the GRE and GMAT are administered by Educational Testing Service. In 2003, Manhattan District Attorney Robert M. Morganthau announced the arrests of eight people in a conspiracy to cheat on the graduate examinations. Morganthau said five of the defendants paid $2,500 each to two men to take the graduate admission tests for them. The two professional test takers were also arrested, as was the man who is alleged to have arranged the scam and provided phony identifications for the test takers so they could get into the classrooms. Some of the students charged

in the case had wanted to attend prestigious New York colleges, including New York University and Baruch College.

Sometimes, parents have become willing conspirators in SAT scams. Although the test is supposed to take between three and four hours, Educational Testing Service will grant extra time — as much as twice the amount of time — to students with learning disabilities, such as dyslexia. To the ordinary student staring at an answer sheet with a blank column, the "Pencils down!" order from the proctor can be devastating. And so, to buy their child more time on the test, some parents are willing to pay whatever it takes to have a psychologist certify that their son or daughter is learning-disabled. Typically, a psychologist may charge as much as $2,400 to examine the student as well as $250 an hour if she is called in to discuss the student's case with an Educational Testing Service representative. On top of the cost, parents must find a psychologist willing to make the diagnosis. Clearly, this is a tactic practiced by only the most affluent parents. Still, wealthy parents are able to find psychologists willing to play ball. A California study found that a quarter of all students approved for learning-disability time extensions on the SAT are from wealthy homes, even though statistics show that just 6 percent of all high school students in America can be considered learning-disabled, and just 13 percent of those students apply for college admission.

Psychologist Jeanne Dietrich, who practices in the upscale New York suburb of White Plains, told the *New York Times* that some parents are very clear about why they are seeking their services: their "child had bombed the SAT" and they think he or she needs more time to do the test on the second try. Another White Plains psychologist, Dana Luck, told the newspaper that parents do not want to know how to treat their child's learning disability, they simply want to know whether the learning disability will qualify

Students have resorted to all sorts of measures in order to cheat, such as typing the answers to potential test questions into graphing calculators or cellular phones before the exam begins.

the student for extra time on the SAT. She said, "It's not, 'Can you help us understand what's wrong with our child?' It's, 'Can you help us document the need for more time on this test.' Students are anxious. Parents are anxious. The environment is anxious."

Risky Behavior

The Gallup Youth Survey wanted to find out how many teens cheat on tests when it polled 1,200 young people between the ages of 13 and 17 in 2003 and 2004. A total of 19 percent of the respondents said "a great deal" of cheating goes on at their schools while 46 percent said "a fair amount" of cheating can be found in their schools. Thirty-four percent said "not very much" cheating goes on. The poll also asked, "Have you, yourself, ever cheated on a test or exam?" Forty-six percent of the respondents admitted to cheating while 53 percent said they had not cheated. Older teens—those aged 16 and 17—were more likely to admit to cheating than teens aged 13 to 15. Furthermore, 53 percent of the older teens said they cheated while 44 percent of the younger students admitted to cheating.

There is no question that cheating is risky behavior, for getting caught could have devastating consequences. Consider what happened to the Saratoga and Landon students as well as the people caught up in the graduate exam scam in New York. It should come as no surprise, then, that the Gallup Youth Survey found that young people who admit to cheating also admit to taking part in other risky behaviors, such as smoking, drinking and eating an unhealthy diet. The 2003 Gallup Youth Survey reported that 72 percent of the teens who said they smoked cigarettes also said they cheated; 66 percent of the teens who said they consumed alcohol admitted to cheating; and 60 percent of the teens who admitted that their diet is "not good" also admitted to cheating.

THE REGULARITY OF CHEATING AMONG AMERICAN STUDENTS

Have you ever cheated on a test or exam?

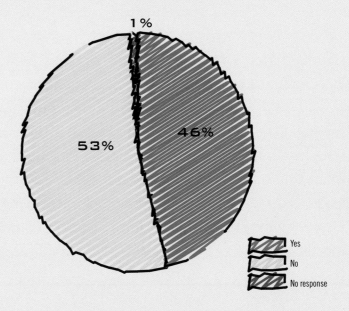

1%

53%

46%

Yes
No
No response

At your school, how common is cheating on tests or exams?

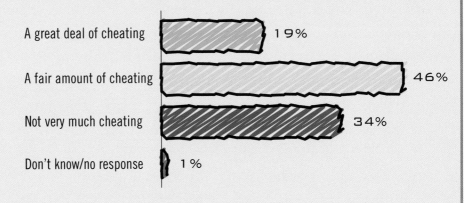

A great deal of cheating — 19%

A fair amount of cheating — 46%

Not very much cheating — 34%

Don't know/no response — 1%

Polls taken January–March 2003 and January–March 2004; 1,985 total respondents (age 13–17)
Source: Gallup Youth Survey/The Gallup Organization

Of course, teenagers may turn to cigarettes, alcohol, and junk food for the same reason they turn to cheating: they are under pressure to get good grades and get into good colleges, and they respond to the pressure by looking for crutches—such as cigarettes, alcohol, junk food, and cheating. Once in college, the students realize the pressure to meet academic standards is even more rigorous than it was in high school, so they continue to practice risky behavior, including cheating. "I cheat because there is a lot of pressure to do well—sometimes I am so busy with a million things, it's like a safety net," an anonymous student told Amanda Munoz, a columnist for the Tufts University student newspaper in Massachusetts. "A lot of pressure is on us, and the stakes are high. People want to do well." Munoz wrote her column shortly after 12 Tufts students were placed on academic probation for cheating in an astronomy class.

The Easy Way Out

One of the nation's foremost experts on cheating is Dr. Donald L. McCabe, founder of the Center for Academic Integrity at Duke University in North Carolina. McCabe's own study into cheating on college campuses polled some 12,000 students at 40 colleges and universities in the United States, and found that nearly 80 percent of undergraduates admit to cheating.

A separate study by McCabe's group polled 4,500 public and private high school students. In that poll, McCabe determined that 74 percent of the students admitted to cheating on tests, 97 percent admitted to cheating when they did their homework, and about half admitted to plagiarism, mostly by cutting and pasting from Internet sources. In the poll conducted among high school students, McCabe asked young people to confess their past trans-

Cheating on standardized tests is difficult—but far from impossible.
Educational Testing Service, which conducts the SAT, says that it invalidates
about 3,000 scores each year because of suspected cheating.

Dr. Donald McCabe has found that some students believe educational strategies like cooperative learning, in which students are permitted to work in small groups to solve problems in the classroom, encourage cheating when students must take tests or solve problems on their own.

gressions, and many responded. "They'd say, 'I did this in ninth grade, and I wish I could do something to rectify it.' You do hear that occasionally," McCabe told a reporter for Gannett News Service.

McCabe added that many students have the attitude that it is the teacher's fault—either the teacher did not do a good job explaining the material, or the teacher did not make himself or herself available for questions. Some students think the system is flawed, that it promotes cheating. McCabe says students have told him that teachers encourage them to work together in groups and solve problems with a team approach; then, the teacher splits everyone up when it is test time. "We do hear that, 'The system is flawed, so it doesn't matter what I do,'" McCabe told the news service.

Finally, some students argue that it is up to the schools and the teachers to make sure students resist the temptation to cheat, or at least do a better job of policing their classrooms so cheating does not occur. McCabe's poll showed that 90 percent of students are aware of cheating in their classrooms, but 32 percent said they had no interest in reporting it.

Some schools have responded. In 1997, Villanova University in Pennsylvania banned the sale of *Cliffs Notes* from the school bookstore. As most English students know, *Cliffs Notes* are study guides to some of the most important and noted works of literature that have been published. Written by literature professors and critics, the study guides point out themes, ideas, and the use of literary devices by the authors that students should know if they are expected to study the books. The company that publishes the guides stresses that they are intended for use by students *after* they read the books. But many busy students look at the novel *Moby Dick* (which spans 595 pages) and the *Cliffs Notes* study guide (which includes just 96 pages) and are tempted to take the easy way out. The *Who's Who* survey determined that some 33 percent of students admitted to reading published study guides instead of the books. Aware of such statistics, Villanova's campus bookstore banned all *Cliffs Notes* study guides under pressure from the faculty. At nearby Swarthmore, Bryn Mawr, and Haverford colleges, administrators said they never permitted *Cliffs Notes* in their schools' bookstores. "I'd rather have them wrestle with the text than succumb to temptation," Swarthmore Associate Dean Robert Gross told the Associated Press.

Regardless of the bans, faculty members wondered whether they would be effective. "To some extent, it's a symbolic stand we're taking," Villanova Vice President for Academic Affairs John Johannes told an Associated Press reporter, "because we know students are still going to get *Cliffs Notes*." Even though the study guides were banned at the bookstores on campus, the guides are still available in private bookstores just blocks away from the schools. And the students may not even find it necessary to leave their dorm rooms in search of a literary study guide; now available on the Internet is Sparknotes.com, essentially a cyber version of *Cliffs Notes*.

Still, at least the faculty members at Villanova were trying. An Oregon State University study found that virtually all cheating on college campuses could be eliminated if professors simply made the

effort. "There is a lot of information out in the popular press about cheating in academia, and most of it tends to place the blame on students," economics professor Joe Kerkvliet said in an Oregon State University news release. "But our research has found that cheating is strongly dependent on what goes on in the classroom. As professors, we can do a lot of things to reduce cheating."

In colleges, it is not unusual for professors to turn over some of the more

A study at Oregon State University found that when a teacher warns students before administering a test that cheating will not be tolerated, instances of cheating are reduced.

mundane duties—such as proctoring tests—to graduate students who are serving as teaching assistants. The Oregon State study found that when teaching assistants administer tests, cheating by students increases by 31 percent. "There are a couple of possible explanations," said Kerkvliet. "One is that teaching assistants have a lot less experience. But it also could be that they are more sympathetic to the students and reluctant to start the whole dirty process of accusing someone of cheating."

Kerkvliet said college professors would do well to distribute multiple versions of the test to ensure that classroom neighbors do not have the same papers in front of them. He also said that a curt verbal warning about cheating just prior to the test is immensely effective. "That surprised me," he said. "I didn't think it would be effective, but professors who state clearly before the exam that cheating will not be tolerated had success in reducing cheating." In fact, Kerkvliet's research showed that a simple verbal announcement admonishing students not to cheat helped reduce cheating in the classrooms by 13 percent. Kerkvliet said that if professors take all the steps he recommends—announce verbal warnings, remain in the classroom during the exam, assign their graduate assistants to be present as proctors as well, and distribute multiple copies of the examination—schools can essentially eliminate cheating on tests.

As many students know, though, cheating goes on in places other than the classroom. It goes on in the library, at home, in dorm rooms—anywhere a student may have access to a computer and the Internet. Moreover, as students also know, cheating happens most often when there is a deadline for a term paper approaching.

Chapter Three

Although the Internet can be a wonderful resource for students seeking information, the abundance of material available makes it easier for students to cheat when they are assigned to write research papers.

Cyber Cheating

Visitors walking onto the campus of the University of Virginia in Charlottesville must pass beneath a brick arch. If those visitors glance up as they approach the arch, they will see these words inscribed in the brickwork: "Enter by this Gateway and Seek the Way of Honor, the Light of Truth, the Will to Work for Men." Those words, by former university president **Edwin Anderson Alderman,** are meant to inspire the students and instill in them the spirit of Thomas Jefferson, the founder of this prestigious university which first opened its doors in 1825.

One way the university has decided to fulfill Jefferson's vision has been to establish an honor code. Before taking a test, each student must certify on the examination that he or she will not cheat. The practice, which was initiated in 1842, is meant to guarantee honesty in the classrooms, but over the years students, faculty members, and school administrators have interpreted the honor code to be in effect anywhere on campus. Students at the University of Virginia take their honor code very seriously; violators of the code can face severe punishment, including expulsion from the university.

In 2001, a student approached Virginia physics professor Louis A. Bloomfield with a complaint: why had he marked her term paper so low while giving high marks to students who handed in plagiarized papers? Bloomfield decided to see if the student's charge was true, so he wrote a software program that would compare similarities in the papers. Checking the papers electronically was possible because for years Bloomfield had required his students to submit their assignments on computer disks. To make the check, Bloomfield simply asked his computer to look for six common words in all his students' term papers. Even so, the plagiarism check would turn out to be no small task. Bloomfield's course is one of the most popular classes at Virginia, with up to 500 students enrolled each semester. To make the checks, Bloomfield ran some 1,800 term papers through the software. It took his computer 50 hours to make all the comparisons.

Bloomfield was shocked by the results. Nearly 160 papers contained similar phrases, sentences, and paragraphs, and when he reviewed those papers individually, he found some papers were complete duplicates of others. University officials suspected that the students plagiarized their papers from Internet sources, in some cases, cutting material out of a World Wide Web page and pasting it verbatim into their term papers. In other cases, it appeared as though term papers were purchased from a number of vendors doing business over the Internet. "I sat there watching the results come in like an election," Bloomfield told the Associated Press. "It was quite clear that people were stealing intellectual information."

A committee of students administers Virginia's honor code. The Honor Committee took nearly two years to investigate the charges, hold trials, and recommend punishments. Many of the students were eventually exonerated of wrongdoing, but in the end 48 students were either expelled or left the college on their own before the committee made recommendations on their cases. "It's never a happy day when 48 students leave, but it shows the system worked," student Christopher Smith, chairman of the Virginia

Word processing programs enable lazy students to cut paragraphs from work published online and paste it into a file they will pass off as their own.

Honor Committee, told a reporter for the Associated Press.

If there is one form of cheating that has come to be more pervasive at high schools and colleges than any other, it is plagiarism. For students who went to school in the 1960s, 1970s, and 1980s, plagiarism could be a long and tedious process that may have been more trouble than it was worth. The plagiarist still had to make a trip to the library and spend time searching the shelves for the appropriate source. Sometimes, there could be a cost involved—coins had to be poured into a copy machine. Since most term papers were produced on typewriters, copying a source meant the information had to be retyped, word for word, into the text of the student's paper. All of that work did not stop students from plagiarizing, but one gets the feeling that if Professor Bloomfield had run a plagiarism check on his students' papers 20 years ago, he may have found one or two cases. But now, thanks to the Internet and the ease of the cut-and-paste command available on word processing programs, plagiarism has grown into epidemic proportions.

Learning Opportunity or Opportunity to Cheat?

In 1998, just 27 percent of U.S. classrooms were wired to the Internet. President Bill Clinton believed many American children were missing the enormous learning opportunities that could be made possible through the Internet. He called on Congress to make funds available to "make it possible for every child with access to a computer to stretch a hand across a keyboard to reach every book ever written, every painting ever painted, every symphony ever composed." Congress responded, and within just three years Internet access was available in 98 percent of public schools.

Not everybody thought it was a good idea. In an essay published in *Time* magazine, Yale University computer science professor David Gelernter prophesized that students would misuse their Internet opportunities. He predicted they would spend valuable classroom time visiting chat rooms with their friends, downloading music, stealing peeks at pornographic sites, and finding other ways to abuse the Internet. "Our children already prefer pictures to words, glitz to substance, fancy packaging to serious content," he wrote. "But the Web propagandizes relentlessly for glitz and pictures, for video and stylish packaging. And while it's full of first-rate information, it's also full of lies, garbage, and pornography so revolting you can't even describe it. There is no quality control on the Internet." Those were legitimate concerns, but even

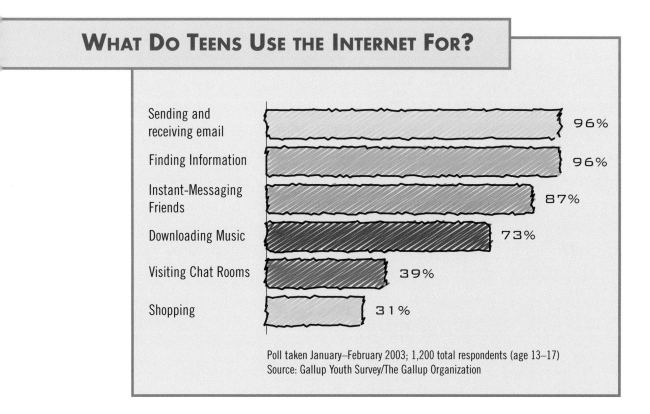

WHAT DO TEENS USE THE INTERNET FOR?

Sending and receiving email — 96%
Finding Information — 96%
Instant-Messaging Friends — 87%
Downloading Music — 73%
Visiting Chat Rooms — 39%
Shopping — 31%

Poll taken January–February 2003; 1,200 total respondents (age 13–17)
Source: Gallup Youth Survey/The Gallup Organization

Gelernter failed to predict one of the main ways students would find to abuse the Internet—plagiarism.

While the schools were being wired for the Internet, so were American homes. By 2003, the Washington-based Pew Research Center reported that 76 percent of U.S. homes were connected to the Internet. A separate study conducted in 2001 by the Pew Research Center said that 94 percent of American students used the Internet for school research. A mere 11 percent of students reported that their only access to the Internet was at school, meaning that a substantial number of the remaining 83 percent were using the Internet to help them with their homework and they were doing it at home—out of view of teachers, school librarians, fellow students, and others in the school community who might be expected to look over their shoulders.

The Gallup Youth Survey's findings support those conclusions. In 2003, The Gallup Organization polled 1,200 young people between the ages of 13 and 17 on their Internet habits. Thirty percent of the respondents said they spend at least five hours a week online, and 96 percent of those students said they use the Internet for finding information. There is no question that students use the Internet for other purposes—87 percent said they use the Internet to chat with friends and 31 percent said they use the Internet to shop. Clearly, though, by 2003 teens recognized the value of the Internet as an educational tool.

Still, by then there was a growing realization by educators and social scientists that the Internet was offering students an easy way to cheat. The 2001 Pew report said:

> The ease of gathering information on the Internet has a darker side. The simplicity of finding out things on the Web also makes it easy for students to cheat. Cutting and pasting text from a Web site and into a paper is effortless.

So is wholesale copying or purchasing finished essays or reports. About a fifth of online youth [18 percent] say they know of someone who has used the Internet to cheat on a paper or test. While 9 percent of those who have been online for a year or less know someone who has cheated, 19 percent of those who have been online for two to three years and 28 percent of those who have been online for more than three years know of people who have used the Net to cheat.

Donald McCabe's research showed Internet plagiarism might even be higher than what the Pew study suggested. McCabe's polling showed that 54 percent of high school students plagiarized by using the Internet; on the college level, 10 percent of students admitted to Internet plagiarism, and 5 percent of students said they turned in pre-written downloaded papers. "I see it as a significant problem at the high school level and a growing problem at the college level," McCabe told the *Denver Post*.

Homework For Sale

Students who wanted to take short cuts were assisted by the growth of two Internet institutions in the 1990s and early 2000s: one legitimate, the other of questionable legitimacy.

The legitimate institution is the search engine—the website that enables a student, without charge, to type in a few keywords and within seconds be provided with dozens, if not hundreds or thousands of links to sources. Search engines such as Google became very sophisticated, enabling students to largely dispense with the fodder of the Internet and concentrate on the truly important sources they would need for their term papers. However, in the hands of a student with intentions to plagiarize, Google could become an indispensable weapon. Now, if a student needed to augment a term paper with a few sentences or paragraphs supporting his argument, Google could provide a quick way to find what he needed. In an essay published in the *Philadelphia Inquirer*,

A 2009 study by Common Sense Media found that 35 percent of American teenagers have used their cell phones to cheat on tests in school.

Louis Bloomfield said, "Writing is hard work, and all the marvels of modern technology have not made it any easier. Vast resources now lie just keystrokes away, but the basic art of assembling one's thoughts into engaging prose is little changed since the days of paper and pencil . . . Unfortunately, the timeless nature of writing isn't shared by its fraudulent imitation: plagiarism. Nearly as ancient as writing itself, plagiarism adapts quickly to new technology. With a Web full of seemingly ownerless prose, plagiarism is as easy as cut and paste."

The other institution that grew with the Internet was the preponderance of Web-based services providing pre-written term papers. In the beginning, some of these services were actually free, designed and supported by college students who believed they were simply making study aids available to their classmates. One such free service was OPPapers.com, which stood for "Other People's Papers." In a column published in the *Daily Bruin*, the student newspaper of the University of California at Los Angeles, student Jennifer Case wrote about an anonymous student's belief that pre-written term papers provide young people with a perspective that is important to know before they sit down to write their own papers. "I think you should be exposed to all pieces of information you think are important to what you're writing," the student told Jennifer. "If you believe you need to see someone else's paper on the same topic, then you should be able to look at that. It's the same thing with books—sometimes the idea is the same as yours, and you have to buy it in order to read it."

But the irony with free download sites is that students were pretty much getting what they paid for. By 2001, OPPapers.com had an inventory of some 10,000 papers available for free downloading to students. Blaine Vess, a college student who founded OPPapers.com, told the *Denver Post* that in his estimation, 70 percent of the term papers in the inventory were poorly written, and 20 percent of the papers would likely earn a D or F if the students turned them in.

It did not take long for Internet-based term paper mills to turn into profit-making ventures. The 2001 Pew study found several Web sites selling pre-written papers, sometimes for substantial fees. "Essay prices ranged from $15 for a two-page paper on *Romeo and Juliet* to $79.95 for a custom-written, two-page college admission essay," the Pew report said. "Most essay sites charge $9 or $10 per page for generic essays and $15 or $20 per page for custom essays." If a student is paying $100 to $300 a page for a custom-written 10- to 15-page term paper, he or she probably does not intend to use the paper as a study guide.

When Is it Cheating?

The people who are hurt by plagiarized term papers are the same people hurt by other forms of cheating. Perhaps a student who does not plagiarize is competing for an academic honor with a student who does. Perhaps a student who plagiarizes is awarded admission to a competitive college, which has denied admission to an honest student. And, as with other forms of cheating, students rationalize their use of the Internet to plagiarize because they are busy and under pressure to achieve and, of course, because everybody else does it. With plagiarism, though, some educators believe there may be another element involved. Most plagiarists, they say, do not start out intending to plagiarize. The problem is they are not sure where legitimate use of a source ends and plagiarism begins. The students who are plagiarizing today grew up with the Internet, where most everything is free, including various screen savers, software, and video games. Many sites offer photographs of sports heroes and rock stars for free, and even movie trailers can be viewed for free. So why not academic sources? In an interview with the *Newark Star-Ledger*, Donald McCabe explained, "There are some students who believe that if it is on the Internet, it's public information and doesn't need to be cited. I hear that among younger high school students, and it speaks to the fact that we need to help kids understand where they need to be, where to draw that line. When is it research, and when is it cheating?"

High schools and colleges have responded to the plagiarism epidemic. Indeed, some of the schools have found decidedly low-tech ways to combat high-tech plagiarism. For example, many teachers tailor their assignments to be specific to each student, requiring them to write term papers comparing their own lives to characters they may be studying in literature. Some teachers require students to turn in hand-written essays and term papers, thereby making it more trouble to cut and paste someone else's work and pass it off as their own. Some schools have adopted honor codes similar to the University of Virginia's under the theory, perhaps, that while Virginia's code may not have completely prevented plagiarism, it might have given many students a reason not to plagiarize. At Auburn University in Alabama, for example, the school adopted an honor code after students said they simply did not know plagiarism was against the rules. "It was astounding, the number of students who came in with plagiarism cases, predominantly, who said they didn't know," Auburn Academic Honors Committee member Tyler O'Connor told the Associated Press.

Some schools have taken legal action. Boston University sued eight providers of pre-written term papers, alleging the services were guilty of fraud and racketeering for selling term papers to students. All the defendants sold term papers over the Internet, and all posted disclaimers on their Web sites warning students that the term papers were for research purposes only. Robert Smith, an attorney for Boston University, told the Associated Press that the warnings were a "sham" and that the term paper providers "know these papers are intended to be submitted for grades and credit."

One service for detecting plagiarism is Turnitin.com. High schools, colleges, and even professional organizations can subscribe to use Turnitin.com's sophisticated plagiarism-detection software. Teachers submit electronic versions of their students' term papers to Turnitin.com, and each page is compared to millions of books, academic journals, and archived student papers, as well as more than 20 billion documents available on the Internet. If the program

The Internet service Turnitin.com was established to combat plagiarism in high schools and colleges. Teachers submit electronic versions of their students' papers, and a powerful software program checks a database that contains billions of pages of documents, looking for similarities that would indicate that the author's work is not original.

detects plagiarism, the teacher will receive back a color-coded copy of the term paper indicating the passages that are suspected to be copies.

Some schools have adopted a different strategy, giving the students the option of submitting their papers through Turnitin.com. If the student receives back a color-coded copy, he or she knows to make changes. John Barrie, president of iParadigms, the company that developed Turnitin.com, said in an interview with the *Washington Post*, "If a student is caught cheating, there is this unambiguous evidence. Instead of asking a student how they came to write a paper so patently beyond their intellectual ability, I could ask, 'Can you explain why 87 percent of this paper is underlined by this program?'" By 2013, Turnitin.com was reviewing and process-

Students who receive good grades through hard work, rather than by cheating, gain greater satisfaction from their accomplishments.

ing over 80 million papers a year.

Despite these safeguards, plagiarism still occurs—even among students that should be expected to know better. High school teacher Amy Malone of Rockville, Maryland, told the *Washington Post* that two of her honors English students turned in identical essays on the Greek tragedies *Antigone* and *Oedipus Rex*. Malone decided to see if she could find the essay for sale on the Internet; it took just a few minutes. Jenny Cross, assistant dean of admissions at Pomona College in California, told *U.S. News and World Report* that she read the same admissions essay three times on the same day, including one version submitted by a high school valedictorian with an SAT score well into the 1500s. In Montgomery County, Maryland, Springbrook High School English teacher Nancy Absehouse assigned her Advanced Placement students to write an essay on Henry James' *The Turn of the Screw*. When the papers were turned in, several of them contained a similar sentence. Absehouse found the sentence in the Sparknotes.com study guide of James' book. "I wanted them to go through an intellectual exercise, and they just wanted the answer," Absehouse told the *Washington Post*. "By our standards, it's cheating. By theirs, it's efficiency."

At the Massachusetts Institute of Technology (MIT), one of the most prestigious universities in America, Class of 2004 President Alvin M. Lin and Vice President Nikhil S. Gidwani resigned after admitting Lin plagiarized their written campaign platform from former MIT class officers; the school newspaper wryly pointed out that even Lin's letter of resignation contained "exactly the same sentence" that could be found in a speech made by former President Clinton.

As for students, many of them feel uncomfortable with the air of academic suspicion that now hangs over their work. They point out that students are reluctant to turn in cheaters; therefore, teachers have turned to a style of policing students' work that conjures up images of Big Brother, the privacy-invading dictator of George Orwell's novel *1984*. At the University of Virginia, sophomore Chris Reams was asked by the *New York Times* what he thought of the new era of suspicion. "The honor system is like a death penalty," Chris said. "Because it's so severe, if you see cheating, and I have, you're reluctant to report it, so we end up resorting to these spy systems."

Chapter Four

Danny Almonte (left) and other members of the Rolando Paulino All-Stars Bronx Little League baseball team hold keys to New York City during a ceremony honoring the team. Little League officials eventually discovered that Almonte was above the age limit, and that the coaches had cheated by permitting him to play in the 2001 Little League World Series.

Dirty Play

Nearly everyone who watched Danny Almonte pitch was convinced the lanky, hard-throwing boy from the Bronx, New York, had major league potential. Danny could already throw a fastball at 70 miles an hour. The lefty also had a killer slider, an off-speed pitch that can fool batters into thinking it is a fastball. Danny's pitching ability was regarded as the primary reason his team, the Rolando Paulino All-Stars, had made it into the Little League World Series in Williamsport, Pennsylvania.

In fact, in the late summer of 2001, Danny pitched a perfect game against a team from State College, Pennsylvania, meaning that every batter he faced failed to either get a hit or a walk—a rare accomplishment on any level of baseball. Danny's pitching captured the attention of the American people, who tuned into the television coverage of the Little League World Series in record numbers to watch the exploits of the team from the Bronx, most of whom were either immigrants from Latin American countries or the sons of Latin American immigrants. What's more, politicians heaped their praise on the All-Stars. "It's tremendous for the Bronx and for New York City," then-New York Mayor Rudolph Giuliani told the *New York Times* as he settled into his seat in the Williamsport grandstand. "It's great for the kids, and really, it's captured the imagination of New York City." Another big fan was President George W. Bush, who paid a visit to Williamsport during the series, making it a point to meet Danny. Following his meeting with the president, Danny said, "I feel very proud because this is my first time being here at the World Series and everything feels great."

Alas, the story of the Rolando Paulino All-Stars would not have a happy ending. After beating State College, league rules prohibited Danny from pitching in the next game, which was against the Little League team from Apopka, Florida. Without Danny on the mound throwing smoke or fooling batters with his slider, the Apopka team's hitters overwhelmed Rolando Paulino's other pitchers, eventually beating the Bronx team by a score of 8–2. The boys from New York took their loss good-naturedly. They finished third in the Little League tournament, then came home to a ceremony at City Hall where Mayor Giuliani presented them with the keys to the city—an honor often bestowed on local heroes. As for Danny, his future looked bright. Fans were convinced that within a few years, they would see the young man from the Bronx on the mound at Yankee Stadium.

Yet, less than a week after the Little League World Series, the news broke that the Rolando Paulino All-Stars had cheated. League rules specify that the teams must be composed of players who are 11 or 12 years old. Older boys would have an advantage over younger players, because they would be bigger and stronger. In the Dominican Republic, where Danny had been born, government officials announced that a review of birth records indicated he was really 14 years old. A 14-year-old pitcher could throw balls harder than the younger and smaller boys would be capable of hitting, which helped explain Danny's pitching success and his perfect game against State College. "We are certainly saddened and angry that we were deceived," Little League President Stephen D. Keener told the *New York Times*. "In fact, millions of Little Leaguers around the world were deceived, as well as Little League as an organization and the governments of the United States and the Dominican Republic."

The Little League stripped the Rolando Paulino All-Stars of their third-place finish in the tournament, forfeiting all their games to the other teams. Danny Almonte was not singled out for blame, however. League officials believed he was an innocent victim of the ruse, and that his father, coaches, and team officials knew all along that Danny was too old for the team, yet permitted him to play.

Why would people so close to Danny Almonte allow the charade to go on? There is a simple answer. In the United States, the road to fame and riches often leads through sports. Major league pitchers can earn millions of dollars a year. By blowing away the competition on the Little League level and making himself into a national hero, Danny would obviously attract the attention of major league scouts. It is not unusual for baseball teams to award fat contracts and signing bonuses to ballplayers who are still in high school. As the hero of the 2001 Little League World Series, Danny Almonte would have had a head start on the competition.

Cheating in sports is not uncommon. Some of the most outrageous examples of cheating have been perpetrated by athletes or the people who manage, coach, or support them. The list is almost endless. One infamous case of cheating occurred in 1919, when eight players from the Chicago White Sox were alleged to have taken money from gamblers to throw the World Series. More recent cases have included the 1980 Boston Marathon, when women's champ Rosie Ruiz was found to have jumped into the race just a half-mile from the finish and then sprinted to victory, or during the U.S. figure-skating competitions that preceded the 1994 Winter Olympics, when thugs hired by the husband of figure skater Tonya Harding assaulted rival Nancy Kerrigan with a steel bar, hoping to injure the skater's knee. Baseball Hall of Fame pitcher Gaylord Perry admitted to cheating in his autobiography, writing that he threw spitballs, an illegal pitch in which the pitcher doctors the ball with grease or another foreign substance to get it to spin in unusual ways.

Stronger and Faster

In a 2002 interview with *Sports Illustrated*, former baseball star Ken Caminiti admitted that he used anabolic steroids throughout much of his career. "If a young player were to ask me what to do, I'm not going to tell him it's bad," Caminiti said of steroid use. "Look at all the money in the game: you have a chance to set your family up, to get your daughter into a good school . . . So I can't say, 'Don't do it,' not when the guy next to you is as big as a house and he's going to take your job and make the money."

The use of steroids, human growth hormone, and other drugs that can improve an athlete's performance has grown increasingly more common over the past two decades. The rising use of performance-enhancing drugs (PEDs) alarms medical professionals, officials of sports leagues, and political figures. President George

U.S. cyclist Tyler Hamilton won a gold medal at the 2004 Olympics, but he was later accused of cheating to do so. A blood sample taken during the Games indicated he had undergone a procedure known as "blood doping" to improve his performance. Hamilton was initially permitted to keep his medal, but in 2012 the International Olympic Committee officially stripped the cyclist of his gold medal and awarded it to the runner-up, Viatcheslav Ekimov.

W. Bush called on athletes to stop using steroids in his 2004 State of the Union address, saying "the use of performance-enhancing drugs like steroids in baseball, football, and other sports is dangerous, and it sends the wrong message—that there are shortcuts to accomplishment and that performance is more important than character."

Athletes have found that an injection of steroids can make them stronger, faster, and more energetic. "I felt like a kid," Caminiti told *Sports Illustrated*. "I'd be running the bases and think, 'Man, I'm fast!' And I had never been fast. Steroids made me like that. The stronger you get, the more relaxed you get. You feel good. You just let it fly."

A Reward with a Risk

Nevertheless, steroids are also very dangerous and can cause a variety of physical ills that are potentially life threatening. In 1992, former football star Lyle Alzado died of brain cancer at the age of 43. Before his death Alzado came to believe his cancer had been caused by excessive steroid use during his playing career. Caminiti himself died of a sudden heart attack in October 2004; he was just 41 years old. Despite this, many athletes have been willing to take the risk, perhaps because they know others are taking PEDs and they are concerned that they will lose the competitive edge.

Until the early 21st century, testing for steroids in American professional sports was sporadic at best. Some organizations, such as the National Football League, took the issue seriously while others, such as the National Hockey League, all but ignored PED use. The union representing Major League Baseball players resisted steroid testing for years, but in 2004 the union finally agreed to a testing program.

As more pro baseball players submitted to tests, MLB officials started noticing a pattern: many players were already using steroids before they made it to the pros. Many who were caught had started using steroids much earlier—sometimes when they were in college or even high school. A study released around this time by the U.S. Centers for Disease Control and Prevention showed that the number of high school students using steroids had doubled between 1991 and 2003.

It should be noted that during this time, education about steroids was not always available in high school health classes. A 2001 Gallup Youth Survey of 501 teenagers between the ages of 13 and 17 reported that just 59 percent of the respondents received

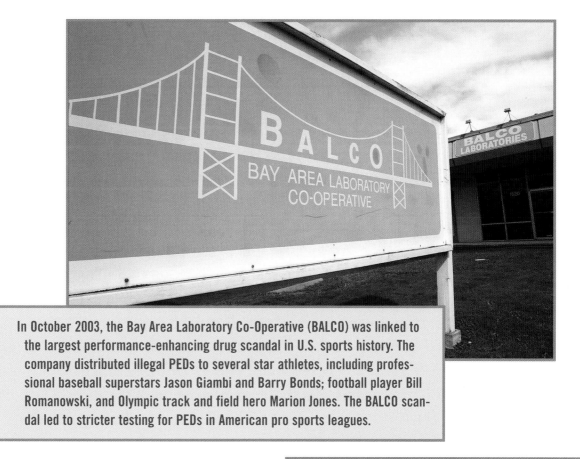

In October 2003, the Bay Area Laboratory Co-Operative (BALCO) was linked to the largest performance-enhancing drug scandal in U.S. sports history. The company distributed illegal PEDs to several star athletes, including professional baseball superstars Jason Giambi and Barry Bonds; football player Bill Romanowski, and Olympic track and field hero Marion Jones. The BALCO scandal led to stricter testing for PEDs in American pro sports leagues.

information on the dangers of steroids in their high school health classes. In contrast, 95 percent of the young people reported learning about drug use in health class, while 92 percent said their health classes covered smoking and 90 percent said they learned about alcohol abuse in health class.

In recent years, many schools have attempted to do more to educate young athletes about the danger of anabolic steroids. One successful program is called Anabolic Steroid Prevention for Teen Athletes (ATLAS). This program provides high school athletes with information about steroid use and and counseling to direct them toward healthy alternatives. In addition, some states have proposed laws requiring high schools to test players for steroids.

Despite this, recent studies show that some high school athletes are still looking for an edge. The 2012 *Monitoring the Future* study, an ongoing survey conducted every two years by the National Institute on Drug Abuse, found that approximately 2 percent of all high school seniors had used steroids at some point in their lives. Another study of young people conducted that year and published in the *Journal of Pediatrics* found the rate of steroid or PED use to be around 5 percent for high school athletes.

Who gets hurt by steroids? For starters, the same type of young people who are hurt by students who cheat on their SAT examinations or plagiarize from the Internet. A football player who does not use steroids may lose out on a college scholarship to another player who may have impressed the college scouts because he seems to be a bit faster and stronger than everybody else. A baseball player on a college or high school team may not be getting a second look from the Major League scout who is more impressed with the slugger with the incredibly big muscles and is willing to overlook the player's runaway acne — a telltale side effect of steroid use. However, the people who are hurt by performance-enhancing drugs include more than just the honest athletes who refuse to cheat. As reported, the steroid taker faces many health risks, both short term and long term. But the steroid user, particularly the young steroid user, is often too blinded by the results—faster speeds in the 40-yard dash, longer home runs, bigger muscles that make protecting the quarterback easier. Jeff Shields, a spokesman for the Pennsylvania Athletic Trainers Society, told the *Lancaster New Era*, "The problem with the high school athlete, like any teenager, is he believes he's indestructible. They live for today and don't think about tomorrow. They need to realize the risk and the reward certainly aren't balanced."

The Gallup Youth Survey has often questioned young people about their attitudes toward sports, including their feelings toward some of the darker sides of sport. In an era when young people are exposed to 24-hour cable TV networks devoted entirely to sports, when the Internet can provide immediate information to satisfy any fan's desire for scores and statistics, and when the news media regularly reports the astronomical salaries paid to stars, the

A young fan sends a message to his favorite players at a baseball game between the New York Mets and San Francisco Giants.

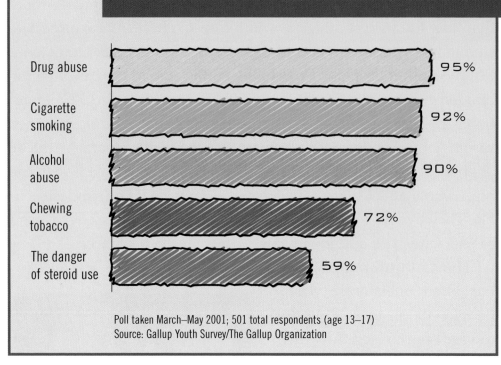

Drug abuse — 95%

Cigarette smoking — 92%

Alcohol abuse — 90%

Chewing tobacco — 72%

The danger of steroid use — 59%

Poll taken March–May 2001; 501 total respondents (age 13–17)
Source: Gallup Youth Survey/The Gallup Organization

Gallup Youth Survey has found that young people are intensely interested in sports and some are looking toward athletics as a career.

In 2001, a survey of 501 teens between the ages of 13 and 17 found that 93 percent of boys and 88 percent of girls have an interest in sports. In addition, a poll taken in 2000 showed that 80 percent of all young people actively participate in sports on some level. Virtually all of the teens who said they play sports reported that having fun is their main motivation, but 72 percent said they participate in sports to increase their chances of getting into college. Certainly, many of those teens have their eyes on athletic scholarships.

Some teens even look on sports as a possible career. In 2003, a Gallup Youth Survey of 1,200 young people found that 5 percent of teens aspire to careers as professional athletes. The survey reported that professional athlete was a much more popular career choice than such common occupations as lawyer (which garnered 4 percent), engineer (3 percent), and chef (3 percent). More boys than girls think they can achieve careers in professional athletics, with 8 percent of the male respondents reporting an interest in playing sports for a living. Just 2 percent of female respondents said they aspire to careers in athletics.

Those numbers clearly reflect the passionate interest of young

Many young people like to play sports in their free time, and hope to make athletics their career. The competition gets much tougher at the college and professional levels, however, so some teens feel they must cheat by taking steroids in order to succeed.

people in sports. Still, young people do realize there is often a seamy side to sports—like steroid use—and some of them admit to being part of that seamy side. In a 2000 poll of 500 young people, 10 percent of the respondents to a Gallup Youth Survey admit-

HOW STEROIDS AFFECT THE BODY

In the United States, steroids cannot be obtained without a doctor's prescription, but anybody who drives across the Mexican border can walk into any drug store in a city like Tijuana and walk out with as many doses of steroids as they can carry. Smuggling them past the U.S. Customs stations can be tricky, but each year tens of thousands of doses make it across the border. Soon, they find their way into American locker rooms, gyms, health clubs, and, ultimately, the bodies of athletes.

Steroids can be taken orally or injected. Once in the body, steroids will be converted into the male hormone testosterone, which helps the body convert protein into muscle mass. Doctors prescribe steroids to patients whose bodies do not produce enough testosterone. A lack of testosterone can cause stunted growth, delayed puberty, impotence, and infertility. In addition, AIDS patients who lose muscle mass because of their disease are often prescribed steroids. The typical male body produces about 10 milligrams of testosterone a day. Athletes who take steroids often take doses that will help them produce hundreds of milligrams. By taking such massive doses athletes can expect to see quick results—within weeks, they will be stronger and faster—but side effects will soon start manifesting themselves as well.

For starters, the body stops producing its own testosterone. The glands that produce testosterone (the testicles) start shrinking and could eventually lose all their ability to produce testosterone. That could lead to a lower sperm count, which could make the steroid user infertile. Therefore, males who use steroids risk losing the ability to father children. Women who take steroids may lose their hair, grow hair in the wrong places, or experience

ted that they were "personally removed from a game for 'playing dirty' or breaking the rules." Boys admitted to breaking the rules more often, with 12 percent owning up to dirty play while 9 percent of the girls said they have broken the rules. According to the survey, older teens were more likely to break the rules, with 13 percent of the 16- and 17-year-old respondents admitting to dirty

(continued on page 70)

menstrual abnormalities. Other side effects of steroid use include: bloating; weight gain; blood-clotting disorders; liver damage; premature heart attacks and stroke; high cholesterol; weak tendons; high blood pressure; addiction dependence; acne; kidney problems; and personality disorders known as "Roid Rage." Teenagers who take steroids face other problems. If they start taking steroids while their bodies are still developing, their bones might stop developing on their own, leaving them shorter than their peers. Steroid use in teens has also led to mental illness.

Another type of performance-enhancing drug, known as human growth hormone, presents its own dangers. Like steroids, human growth hormone is illegal without a prescription. Athletes take it to strengthen their joints. One of the side effects is an enlarged head; baseball players who have taken human growth hormone say they have difficulty getting their batting helmets to stay on. Facial characteristics also change, as brows and jaws become more pronounced.

Athletes who take steroids, human growth hormone, and other PEDs tend to sustain muscle and bone injuries more often than athletes who do not take performance-enhancing drugs. Birmingham, Alabama, sports orthopedist James Andrews told *Sports Illustrated*, "I'm seeing four to five times as many of these injuries as I did just 10 years ago—and I'm seeing them in younger and younger athletes. If the pros are doing it, the college kids aren't far behind, and the high school and junior highs are right behind them. I try to counsel them, but it is a secret box that they find themselves in, and they don't want to talk to me about it."

Teen Views on Pressure

Do you feel that coaches apply too much pressure to win?

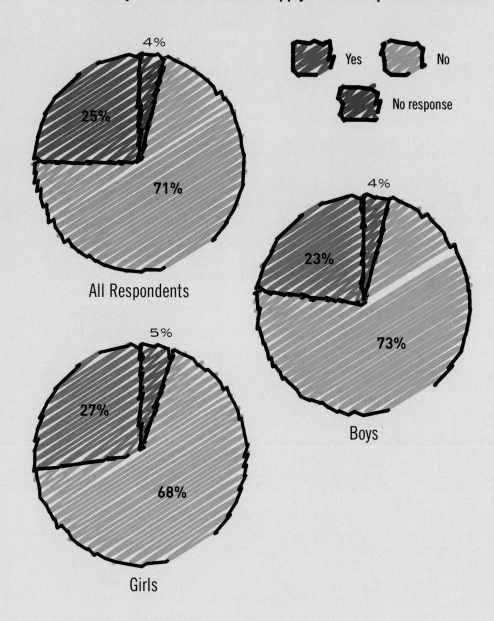

Yes

No

No response

All Respondents
- 4%
- 25%
- 71%

Boys
- 4%
- 23%
- 73%

Girls
- 5%
- 27%
- 68%

Polls taken July–October 2000; 500 total respondents (age 13–17)

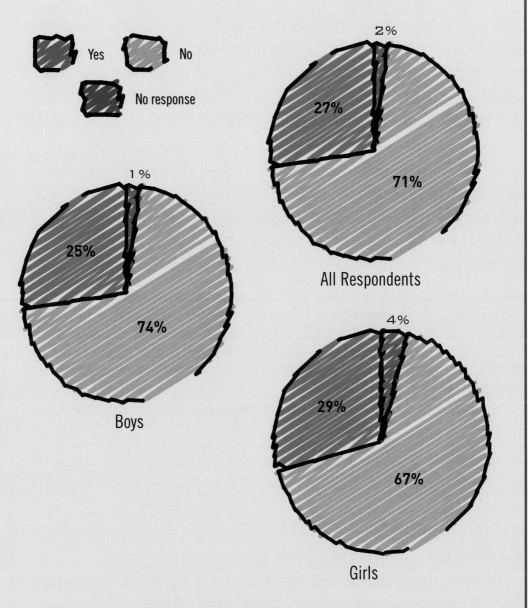

Do you feel that parents apply too much pressure to win?

Yes

No

No response

2%

27%

71%

All Respondents

1%

25%

74%

Boys

4%

29%

67%

Girls

Source: *YouthViews: The Newsletter of the Gallup Youth Survey*, February 2001/The Gallup Organization

play, while just 9 percent of the teens between 13 and 15 reporting that they break the rules.

Pressure from the Outside

Some teens blame their coaches and parents for encouraging them to win at any cost. A 2001 Gallup Youth Survey of 500 teens found that 25 percent of young athletes believe coaches "apply too much pressure to win" while 27 percent said their parents pressure them too much to win. Felipe Almonte, who was accused of falsifying his son Danny's birth records, may fall into the category of the parent willing to bend the rules to win. Somebody else who might fit that description was Robert Lange Sr., the uncle of 1973 All-American Soap Box Derby champ Jimmy Gronen. The Soap Box Derby is an annual event held in Akron, Ohio, in which competitors build small racing cars that dash downhill, powered by gravity alone. An accomplished engineer, Lange admitted to doctoring his nephew's car by installing a battery and electromagnet, which gave it an extra push at the start of the race. In the end, Jimmy was stripped of his trophy and Lange faced criminal charges.

And there is no question that coaches sometimes play dirty. In recent years the NCAA, which oversees college athletics, has imposed sanctions on a number of high-profile college football programs. One was Ohio State, which was prohibited from playing in postseason bowl games in 2012 due to recruiting violations. Recruiting violations have also been investigated at the University of Miami, Oregon State, and other top football programs.

In 2003, the University of Georgia fired basketball coach Jim Harrick after an internal investigation showed three players had received A's in a class they did not regularly attend. The class, titled "Coaching Principles and Strategies of Basketball," was taught by Harrick's son, an assistant coach for the basketball team. An easy A can always come in handy for players who must typically maintain a C average in order to keep their eligibility to play interscholastic sports.

Cheating scandals in college sports surface quite frequently. Over the years, players at Northwestern University, Boston College, the University of Kentucky, and City College of New York, among others, have been implicated in scandals to fix the outcomes of games. Consider the case of Stevin "Headache" Smith, a star shooting guard on the 1994 basketball team of Arizona State University. Smith was headed for an NBA contract worth millions of dollars, but while going to school he struck up a friendship with Benny Silman, an Arizona State student who ran a small-time bookmaking business on campus. Typically, gamblers place bets based on the "line" or "point spread" of a particular game. They are not too concerned with who wins or loses, but rather with how many points separates the winning score from the losing score. Silman started paying Smith to shave points, meaning Headache was to do what he could to ensure that the final score of the game—and therefore the point spread—ended where Silman wanted it to end. To do this Smith purposely missed shots, tossed wild passes at his teammates, or turned the ball over to opponents.

At first, the scheme remained small-time, but soon some big-time gangsters found out about it. Authorities knew the games were rigged when Las Vegas casinos started receiving bets on Arizona State games totaling hundreds of thousands of dollars. Silman and Smith were arrested and convicted; Silman went to jail for four years, and Smith for a year. After his release, Headache

Smith found a place on a professional basketball team in France, earning a salary considerably lower than he could have expected in the NBA.

Smith told an interviewer for ESPN that point-shaving in college basketball is common and that the temptations for easy money are often impossible to resist, particularly for poor inner city kids. "You ask me do I think it's going on?" Smith said. "Yes, it's going on . . . You take a young person out of a low income area and you present, you know, a stack of hundreds to him and it's not like you're killing nobody or nothing. How many of them do you think are going to say no?"

A similar point-shaving scandal occurred during the 2009-10 college basketball season, when University of San Diego star point guard Brandon Johnson helped to fix at least four games. He would miss a foul shot or throw a bad pass at a key time to ensure that his team would not cover the spread. According to an FBI investigation, the gamblers who paid Johnson cleared some $120,000 in winning bets on the fixed games. Johnson was paid $1,000 per game—not much, considering that he was eventually caught, convicted, and in March 2013 was sentenced to six months in a federal prison.

Chapter Five

In this scene from a 2004 commercial for Pepsi and the iTunes Music Store, Annie Leith asserts her right to download music off the Internet. The issue of music piracy is complex; some musicians complain that they are being cheated by Internet file sharing, but others argue that downloading songs actually helps record sales.

Music Piracy

Fans tuning into the 2004 Super Bowl may have seen a TV commercial for the soft drink Pepsi-Cola featuring 14-year-old Annie Leith of Staten Island, New York. In the ad, while the group Green Day plays its version of the 1966 hit "I Fought the Law," Annie hoists a bottle of Pepsi, smiles at the camera and says, "We're still going to download music free off of the Internet and there's not a thing anyone can do about it."

What Annie did not mention in the ad, though, is that she planned to use the fee she earned for appearing in the commercial to pay a $3,000 court settlement levied against her for illegally downloading music from the Internet. Annie was one of 261 defendants named in a wave of lawsuits filed in the fall of 2003 by the Recording Industry Association of America (RIAA), the trade group that represents the major music recording companies. According to the suits, each of the defendants downloaded and distributed at least 1,000 songs they obtained for free in violation of the copyright on each song. Not only did Annie and the others face civil court penalties for downloading music, if prosecutors really wanted to get tough with them the teenagers could have been arrested and charged with federal copyright infringement crimes that are punishable by fines totaling $250,000 and prison terms as long as three years. "Nobody likes playing the heavy and having to resort to litigation," RIAA President Cary Sherman said in a statement, "but when your product is being regularly stolen, there comes a time when you have to take appropriate action. We simply cannot allow online piracy to continue destroying the livelihoods of artists, musicians, songwriters, retailers and everyone else in the music industry." Following the initial 261 lawsuits, the RIAA continued to file cases against defendants. By early 2004, nearly 2,000 illegal music downloaders—many of them teenagers—had been named as defendants by the RIAA.

"I didn't think it was that big of a deal to download music," 17-year-old Kristina Maalouf of Concord, California, told the *San Francisco Chronicle*. "Everybody I know was downloading music. It was all around. I heard everyone talking about it." Kristina and her 14-year-old sister Michelle were also named as defendants in suits by the RIAA. The two girls joined Annie Leith and other teens in the Super Bowl commercial.

The purpose of the commercial was to advertise a new promotion by the soft drink maker, giving away 100 million free download codes under Pepsi bottle caps. To make the offer, Pepsi struck a deal with the Apple iTunes Music Store, which charges a fee to music downloaders and pays royalties to the record companies as well as the artists who write and perform the music. And so, when Annie Leith told Super Bowl viewers that she still intended to download music for free, what she really meant is that the music would be free as long as Pepsi was giving away download codes under its bottle caps. Otherwise, each song would cost 99 cents. "It's all in good spirit," Pepsi-Cola spokesman Dave Burwick told *USA Today*, in explaining the intent of the Super Bowl commercial. "This has been a huge cultural phenomenon. It's highly relevant and topical for consumers. We're turning people to buy music online vs. stealing it online."

There is no question that people who find a way to download free music are stealing it. Just ask the teenagers in Pepsi's Super Bowl commercial. Still, many young people who admit to downloading music wonder what all the fuss is about. Aren't big-time rock stars wealthy? Don't the recording companies have lots of money? "I see nothing wrong with it," 17-year-old Somers, New

During the Pepsi–iTunes promotion, purchase of Pepsi products provided an access code that could be used to download songs, which ordinarily sold for 99 cents on the iTunes Music Store.

York, student Peter Silberman told the *Journal News* of White Plains, New York. "I think the record industry has gotten greedy."

It may seem that way on the surface, but when people steal music, they do more than just cheat big recording stars like Jay-Z or Avril Lavigne or OutKast or the large corporations that own the labels. They also cheat the engineers who record the music, the compact disk manufacturers, even the record store clerks. And some say people who download music illegally are cheating new artists as well. The record company may not give this artist a chance to make a second CD. Lars Ulrich, drummer for the heavy metal band Metallica, told *USA Today*, "It's not the Metallicas and Madonnas and Linkin Parks and Bruce Springsteens that take the hardest hit, it's the 10 developing bands each label has on its roster every month. That gets trimmed to three. Instead of getting $1 million to make videos and tour, you go home if nothing happens in the first five minutes of that project. Young artists won't have a chance."

In 2001, the RIAA won a court ruling shutting down the file-sharing feature of the Internet-based music provider known as Napster. The company, which had been founded in 1999 by college dropout Shawn Fanning, enabled music fans to share digital music files. Napster kept no digital music files of its own; instead, for a fee the company provided what is known as a "peer-to-peer" link to its customers. By going through Napster's Web page, a fan could search the hard drives of other members' computers to find the songs he or she wanted to download.

Internet Underground

Music found its way onto the Internet in the 1990s. Although the Internet existed before then, few people had access to it, and it was difficult for those that did to obtain music in a digital format.

For starters, there simply was not that much music available. Computers were also far more primitive than they are today, and lacked the storage capacity and processing ability to handle the large amounts of digital information that a song required. Finally, modem speeds were slower than they are today. Even if a music fan could find his song and shoehorn it onto his hard drive, it might have taken an hour or more to download the tune.

Things began changing as computers became more powerful and modem speeds became faster. Another element was an improved ability to compress digital files. In the late 1980s, German computer scientists had developed the MP3 compression program, which enabled digital music files to become smaller without a noticeable loss in sound quality. In the mid-1990s Manufacturers began adding CD players—and soon CD burners—to computers, which enabled fans to copy their downloaded songs onto their hard drives, or make copies of their compact disks. In 1998, a program that played MP3 files, called "Winamp," was offered for download on the Internet as a free music player. Soon, people all over the world were copying music files off of CDs and converting them to MP3 files, then making them available to others over the Internet for download.

By this time the music industry had discovered the World Wide Web. Retailers attempted to sell CDs over the Internet, sometimes even giving fans a sample of the music online to entice them to buy the albums. Rock stars established their own Web pages or encouraged their fans to create tribute sites for them. To help out their fans, many rockers supplied the photos, insider news, tour gossip, and, of course, music samples to post on the Web. Members of the Beastie Boys were particularly generous, using their fans' tribute sites to promote their concerts.

By the time Napster arrived on the scene in 1999, there were tens of thousands of songs already available online. Napster was an instant success, mainly because the program made it so easy to find and download free music. By the summer of 2000—not even a year after Napster's startup—the Internet research company Media Metrix reported that some 5 million people a month were logging onto Napster. A year later, there were 65 million registered users of Napster, all sharing files and listening to each other's music (many mixing their own CDs), none paying royalties to the copyright holders. *USA Today* reported that 1.7 billion blank CDs were sold in 2002, a 40 percent increase over 2001. Meanwhile, worldwide music sales dropped by nearly 7 percent in 2002.

It did not take long for people in the music industry to figure out what was going on. The rock band Oasis repeatedly sent its lawyers to court to shut down Internet sites that were posting and distributing copyrighted material, including the band's songs. In late 1999, members of Metallica were working on music for a movie soundtrack, which was to include the song "I Disappear." The frustrated rockers spent months in the studio, recording and re-recording the song, struggling to produce a version they thought could be released. While working on the song, band members discovered, much to their astonishment, that no fewer than three versions of "I Disappear" were already available online and being traded over Napster. In fact, Metallica's members discovered that all their songs were available through Napster's peer-to-peer file sharing, and they were not collecting a dime in royalties for them. Metallica and other music stars sued Napster. So did the RIAA.

Throughout the music world, recording artists complained loudly about what was going on. The rapper Eminem griped that songs from his album *The Marshall Mathers LP* were available for trade on Napster weeks before the CD was scheduled to arrive in the stores. "If you can afford a computer, you can afford to pay $16 for my CD," Eminem fumed in author John Alderman's book, *Sonic Boom*. By mid-2001, Napster was under court order to drop its peer-to-peer file-sharing feature.

Once Napster was out of the peer-to-peer business, fans found other ways to share music files for free. They made use of such programs as Kazaa, Morpheus, and Grokster to carry on peer-to-peer trading, swapping music files in a sort of Internet underground. David Callahan, author of *The Cheating Culture*, estimated that following the Napster peer-to-peer shutdown, more than 100 million people had downloaded Kazaa world-

Roger McGuinn of the Byrds (seated left) and Metallica drummer Lars Ulrich (center) argue with Hank Barry, CEO of Napster, during a July 2000 hearing on musical copyright and the Internet before the Senate Judiciary Committee. In 2001 the music industry won a court ruling that forced Napster to pay artists when songs are downloaded.

During the mid-1990s, the Beastie Boys were one of many groups that worked with their fans to establish tribute websites on the Internet, which helped to promote their concerts. The band also offered high-quality MP3 audio files of its songs on its official website for free download, but by the end of 1998 its label, Capitol Records, had replaced the MP3s with lower-quality audio files. "It boggles my mind that labels are freaked and afraid, instead of really getting involved with what's going on," Beastie Boy Mike D told the *Wall Street Journal*.

wide. "There are now several million people engaged in music file swapping at any given moment of any day, and it's estimated that 2.6 billion music files are downloaded every month, mostly in a way that is a federal felony," wrote Callahan. "Surveys show that nearly 50 percent of teenagers and a quarter of all Americans have downloaded music in the past month. Forty-two percent of admitted music pirates report having copied a CD rather than buying it."

Right Or Wrong? (It Depends on Who You Ask)

The Gallup Youth Survey has reported widespread music piracy by young people. From December 2000 through February 2001, while Napster was still enabling its users to share files, a Gallup Youth Survey of 501 young people between the ages of 13 and 17 reported that 81 percent were aware of Napster. Of those teens, 93 percent said they knew of friends who downloaded music for free. While Napster was in the peer-to-peer business, Shawn Fanning argued that file-sharing could enhance CD sales by promoting individual songs. Teens who responded to the Gallup Youth Survey disagreed; 55 percent said they believed people would be less likely to buy CDs if the music were available for free over the Internet.

In early 2003, more than a year after Napster dropped its file-sharing feature, the Gallup Youth Survey asked 1,200 young peo-

The success of Napster spawned dozens of imitators, so music downloads continued even after the Napster site was shut down in 2001.

Moral Acceptibility of Downloading Music for Free

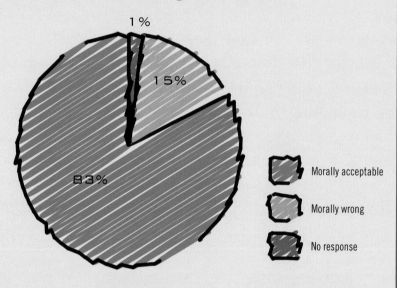

1%

15%

83%

- Morally acceptable
- Morally wrong
- No response

Do Music Downloads Affect Sales?

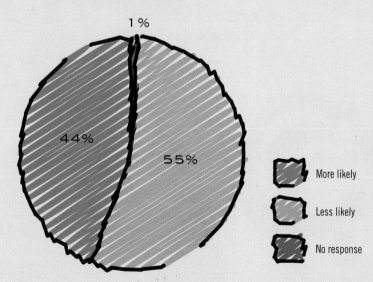

1%

44%

55%

- More likely
- Less likely
- No response

Polls taken December 2000–February 2001; 501 total respondents (age 13–17)
Source: *YouthViews: The Newsletter of the Gallup Youth Survey*, Feburary 2001/The Gallup Organization

ple whether they download music from the Internet. A total of 47 percent of the respondents reported that they continued to seek free music on the World Wide Web. Gallup researchers reported the comments of some typical teen respondents: "It's so much more convenient than having to buy a CD—especially if you only like one song on the whole album," a high school senior named Mary told the Gallup Organization. "You can do it for free and save yourself 16 bucks and a car ride." New York City high school junior Ben told Gallup researchers, "File-sharing is great because unknown artists get to be heard, you can hear the music before you buy it and it's totally free." When the Gallup Organization asked a 17-year-old music downloader named Elza whether she knew she was breaking federal law by sharing music files online, she responded, "I hate to say it, but I don't think about that much. [File sharing] is so popular that no one seems to ever have a problem with it."

The survey reported that boys are more likely than girls to download music; 52 percent of the male respondents and 43 percent of the female respondents said they swap music files online. As for the racial composition of file-sharers, 53 percent of white teens said they download music, compared with 38 percent of nonwhite teens who said they seek free music online.

As teens continued to download music, The Gallup Organization wanted to know whether young people considered file-sharing to be similar to cheating. A clear majority did not. In a Gallup Youth Survey of 1,200 teenagers conducted in August 2003, 83 percent of the respondents said they believe it is "morally acceptable" to download music from the Internet. In contrast, just 18 percent of teens said they found cheating on a test to be morally acceptable.

Even those who admitted that they knew illegally download-ing music was wrong planned to continue doing it. One respon-dent, a 15-year-old named Brad, told the Gallup Organization, "Downloading music is theft and theft is morally wrong. Just because you're not walking into a store and grabbing a CD from the shelf, it's still wrong. It's hurting the record industry and the artists who make the music. But will it stop me from download-ing? No way."

It could be argued that teenagers do not feel they face a moral dilemma about downloading music because music has, in a way, been free for years. After all, anybody can turn on the radio at any time and listen to music free of charge, 24 hours a day. Perhaps teens might have trouble drawing the line between what has always been free on the radio and what they think should be free on the Internet. Elizabeth, a 17-year-old Gallup respondent, said, "I think downloading music from the Internet is morally accept-able because it's the same thing as taping a song from the radio— no one is getting hurt. But cheating on a test is getting help from an outside source without studying and learning the material. So you're not only harming yourself, but possibly your classmates, as well, by creating a false curve."

Elizabeth may not be making a fair comparison. Music may be free on the radio to listeners, but radio stations do pay royalties to play the songs. To a radio station, the music is programming—the material it needs to fill time on its broadcast band so that people will listen to the station. The radio station makes its money by sell-ing advertising to businesses interested in marketing their goods and services to the people likely to be listening to the radio station.

For years radios have been equipped with cassette tape recorders that permit the listener to record music or any other type of programming. Federal copyright law does not prohibit taping off the radio, however, because the listener is making the tapes for personal use. The listener does not intend to make the song or program available for mass distribution over the Internet or, as in Napster's case, facilitating its availability to others for a fee.

Still, just as with cases of term paper plagiarism from Internet sources, teenagers may have difficulty understanding that not everything on the Internet is free for the taking. "I suspect the largest moral issue is simply the old beach-combing, law-of-the-sea, finders keepers mentality," said Rushworth Kidder, president of the Institute for Global Ethics in Camden, Maine. "[Teens think,] 'If something falls overboard into the great sea of the Internet and washes up on my computer—hey, it's there, isn't it? If those guys really wanted to restrict its usage, they should tie down their cargo more tightly. Not my fault I stumbled onto it.'"

In 2012, the Nielsen Company released the "Music 360 Report," a comprehensive study of music listening and purchasing habits in the United States. The report suggested that illegal downloading of music is no longer epidemic. Just 17 percent of teens, the report revealed, engage in online music sharing. This is probably attributable to various factors. First, the successful legal campaigns against file-sharing sites like Napster. Additionally, the cost of paid music downloads—$0.69 to $1.29 per song on iTunes, for example—strikes many people as reasonable. Finally, services that stream music (such as Pandora and Spotify), often for a small subscription fee, are an attractive option for many music-loving teens.

Chapter Six

President George W. Bush meets elementary school students as part of a character education event in the White House. Thanks to high-profile cases of cheating, many schools and colleges are placing a new emphasis on teaching ethics.

Ethics Pays

Robert Cohen and Fred Dellorfano are only too delighted to lecture college students about business ethics. On occasion, the two men have been asked to speak to young people on such issues as whether they should use a company's e-mail for personal messaging, whether to use a photocopying machine at work to print their own résumés, and whether to accept a job with a company they suspect may be breaking the law.

Cohen and Dellorfano have a lot of experience in such matters. For starters, they are both former attorneys. Also, both men are convicted felons who were sentenced to lengthy prison terms on fraud charges. To speak to the classes, prison officials transport Cohen and Dellorfano to college campuses where they deliver their lectures to students preparing for careers in corporate America. Following their talks to the students, the two men are whisked back to Allenwood Federal Prison in Pennsylvania.

"Nearly 40 years ago I was in your position," Dellorfano told a class of students from Susquehanna University in a lecture reported in the *Christian Science Monitor*. "I was brought up in a wonderful, moral-type family situation. I had everything. What would have caused me to fall off the edge?"

The talks given by the two convicted felons are not unlike the so-called "Scared Straight" programs offered to juvenile offenders. In those programs, teenagers heading toward a life of crime are lectured by prison inmates serving lengthy sentences for violent offenses, such as murder, rape, and robbery. After getting a tour of the cold and forbidding prison, the young delinquents are told about the harsh realities of spending the rest of their lives behind bars in a maximum-security institution.

Cohen and Dellorfano were not sentenced to serve their terms among violent criminals in a tough maximum-security jail. Allenwood is a minimum-security institution. All the inmates are nonviolent offenders, and most were professionals convicted of so-called "white collar" crimes such as embezzlement, tax evasion, and insider trading. Instead of cells, inmates live in dormitories, and there are no bars on the doors. Inmates at Allenwood are given a certain amount of freedom that prisoners in maximum-security institutions do not enjoy. Still, as Cohen and Dellorfano stand in front of the business students dressed in their rumpled prison-issue clothes and talk of being separated from their families for a decade or more, the two men do make an impression. Susquehanna accounting professor Richard Davis told the *Christian Science Monitor*, "I can stand up and talk about white-collar crime and say: 'Be good, be ethical' and all of that. But when I'm doing it, it's like preaching, and [the students] don't get it from the horse's mouth."

Susquehanna is not the only college that now requires business students to sit through lectures delivered by white-collar criminals. At the University of Maryland, students are given a tour of a federal prison and a chance to talk with former executives, attorneys, and accountants doing time for cheating, swindling, and stealing. At Pepperdine University in California, the education of business students typically includes a tour of a high-tech company located in the state's prosperous Silicon Valley where they will meet entrepreneurs. Next, they will visit the financial district of downtown San Francisco and speak with bankers and financiers. Finally, they will tour Lompac Federal Prison, where they will also meet entrepreneurs, bankers, and financiers. "We want them to see the dark side, and we want them to see ethics pays," Pepperdine finance professor Jim Martinoff told the *San Francisco Chronicle*.

Many colleges have realized that while they may do a very good job of teaching students how to market products, make profits, and balance budgets, they have not been doing a good job teaching them how to be honest. And so they have added business ethics courses to their curriculums. High schools are also thinking hard about how they have been teaching morals and ethics to young people, and "character education" is now very much a part of the program at many schools.

But why do schools have to teach students not to cheat? Hasn't that always been a lesson best learned at home? Or at church? During the 1960s public schools were told *not* to teach moral behavior, the result of a U.S. Supreme Court order forbidding Bible readings and any other form of religious instruction in public schools. To ensure that schools did not violate the Supreme Court order, administrators told teachers to stick to history, mathematics, English, and other academic subjects. Thus, for decades lessons in ethics have been left to parents and religious leaders. Judging by the number of students who admit to cheating, however, perhaps parents and churches could use some support in their efforts to enforce moral behavior.

Code of Silence

The divorce rate in American society is staggering. According to the 2000 U.S. Census, roughly half the couples that get married in the United States get divorced. That means there are a lot of teenagers who leave school every day and go home to a household where there is only one parent. As such, there is just one adult in the household to counsel the children about moral behavior and how to handle ethical dilemmas that may lead to cheating. Over the years, there have been numerous studies into the effects of divorce on children. Many of them have suggested that children of divorced parents are more at risk for doing poorly in academics and exhibiting anti-social behavior than children who grow up in two-parent households. For example, a 1998 study by the Washington-based Center for Law and Social Policy said:

> Children with divorced parents are more likely to exhibit signs of early disengagement from school than children from intact families. Marital disruption is accompanied by increases in truancy and more negative attitudes toward school. Marital disruption appears to be associated with behavioral and affective changes, rather than with changes in more cognitive phenomena like aspirations and grades. Children of divorce report lower educational expectations on the part of their parents, less monitoring of school work by both their mothers and fathers, and less overall supervision of school and social activities than children from intact families.

Of course, not all young people who cheat live in one-parent homes. Jonathan Lebed, who concocted the scheme to cheat investors on the Internet, lived in a two-parent home. Many of the plagiarists who dropped out of the University of Virginia during the school's cheating scandal returned to two-parent homes. Many of the teenagers sued by the Recording Industry Association of America for illegally downloading music had to explain to their mothers *and* fathers what they had done wrong. Nevertheless, there is no question that teenagers crave moral guidance at home, and young people who grow up in single-parent households wish their mothers and fathers would have tried harder to make their marriages work. In 2003, the Gallup Youth Survey asked 1,200 young people between the ages of 13 and 17 this question: "Generally speaking, do you think it is too easy or not easy for people in this country to get divorced?" Seventy-seven percent of the respondents said it is too easy for parents to get divorced. Clearly, most of those respondents living in single-

Studies indicate that children who come from broken homes are at greater risk of doing poorly in school.

parent homes were dreaming of a home life where mom and dad are always available as sounding boards—adults they can go to when they need to talk about what is right and wrong.

Since many teens do not always have easy access to their mothers and fathers, they bounce ideas off each other. Good friends are important, but they may not always give the best advice. A Gallup Youth Survey conducted among 500 young people in 1988 said that 38 percent of teens discuss what is "right or wrong" with their friends. No doubt, some of the advice they often give each other is wrong—and that advice is often to keep your mouth shut. In fact, most teenagers are not willing to report wrongdoing to teachers, police and their parents, maintaining an unofficial code of silence. When it comes to cheating, rare is the student who will take the initiative to identify the cheaters to his teacher.

According to security expert Wolfgang W. Halbig, the existence of this code of silence should come as no surprise to certain groups, including parents, school administrators, school board members, legislators, and law enforcement officials. In an essay published in the *American School Board Journal*, Halbig wrote:

> I have been an assistant principal, a teacher and a coach, a state police officer and a director of school district security. In all those roles, I saw how and why a code of silence is so deeply ingrained in youth culture. Historically, students have been loath to "tattle," "rat" or "narc" on their peers—especially in secondary grades when social acceptance often overrides the urge to do the right thing. Added to that is the fear of violent retribution for turning someone in that is probably more real today than ever before.

Actually, the code of silence may not be as rock-solid as it used to be. Following the 1999 murders of students at Columbine High School in Colorado, many students realized that their lives could be in danger if they kept silent when they were aware trouble was brewing. In 2002, the National Association of Students Against

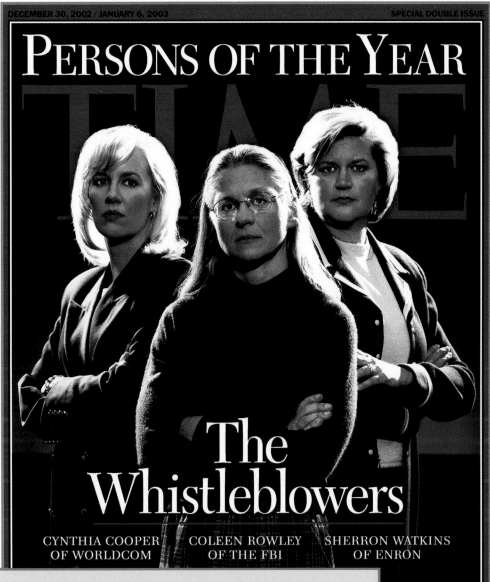

DECEMBER 30, 2002 / JANUARY 6, 2003   SPECIAL DOUBLE ISSUE

PERSONS OF THE YEAR

The Whistleblowers

CYNTHIA COOPER   COLEEN ROWLEY   SHERRON WATKINS
OF WORLDCOM   OF THE FBI   OF ENRON

The code of silence exists in the corporate world as well as in the classroom, and many people are unwilling to speak out when they see their bosses or peers cheating to gain a business advantage. Those who do speak out may be ostracized by coworkers, but they may also be praised for their courage, as were Cynthia Cooper, Coleen Rowley, and Sherron Watkins, each of whom revealed corrupt or dishonest practices in the organizations where they worked.

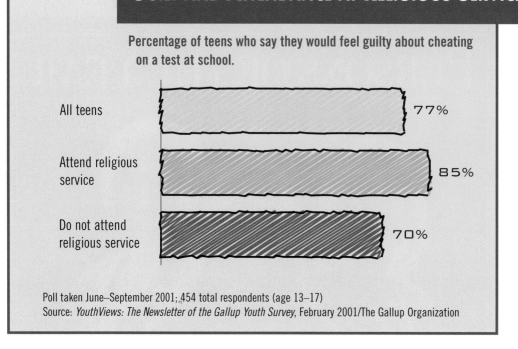

GUILT AND ATTENDANCE AT RELIGIOUS SERVICES

Percentage of teens who say they would feel guilty about cheating on a test at school.

All teens — 77%

Attend religious service — 85%

Do not attend religious service — 70%

Poll taken June–September 2001; 454 total respondents (age 13–17)
Source: *YouthViews: The Newsletter of the Gallup Youth Survey*, February 2001/The Gallup Organization

Violence Everywhere (SAVE) released a study that said in light of the Columbine massacre, 81 percent of students are more willing to break the code of silence than they were before. Of course, that study was geared to finding out whether students would break the code of silence to prevent violence. It remains to be seen whether young people feel just as strongly about reporting cheating.

Ethics and a Higher Authority

Considering all the world's major religions teach lessons about honesty, if advice on ethics is not always available at home, surely young people can learn their moral lessons in church. The problem, however, is that many teenagers do not show up for the sermon or, if they do, they are not listening to what the spiritual leader of the congregation has to say.

The Gallup Youth Survey has often gauged young people's interest in religious activity. A poll conducted among 454 young people in 2001 revealed that less than half of American teenagers had attended church in the preceding seven days. And for the minority of American teenagers who do find their way to religious services, it is difficult to say whether they are paying a great deal of attention. According to the Gallup Youth Survey, 84 percent of church-going teens could recall the last sermon they heard, but 55 percent of them could not recall the *message* of the sermon. In other words, if the minister, priest, rabbi, or imam told them that honesty is a virtue, it is likely the message would not stick.

This is unfortunate because the Gallup Youth Survey shows that teenagers who pay attention to what they hear in church lead healthier lives, both physically and mentally. The poll, taken among 501 young people in 2001, assessed teens' health habits, such as whether they smoke cigarettes, eat well, and participate in regular health checkups. Teenagers who describe themselves as religious were found to generally have good health habits—66 percent of them fell into a "good health habits" group. What's more, the survey found, "Teens with good habits are more likely to believe 'God gives us strength to deal with problems, to call on our God-given resources, and to draw on our inner strength' than teens with poor habits." It seems that when religious teens need a sounding board to answer questions about ethics and mother and father are not available, they find themselves able to consult with a higher authority.

Character Education

With just a minority of teens getting their "moral compasses" adjusted at home or at church, schools in the United States are finding they have to step in. "The trend now is that there is no one else to turn to for the teaching of right and wrong so the schools are being asked to take it on," Samuel G. Sava, executive director of the National Association of Elementary School Principals, told the *New York Times*. As such, character education programs have been started in a number of schools. The U.S. Department of Education has promoted the concept, making millions of dollars available in annual grants to schools that establish character education programs. Students also endorse the concept, And young people may, in fact, be ahead of the curve in supporting ethics training in school. In 1993 (long before the concept of character education was introduced in the schools) the Gallup Youth Survey conducted a poll showing that 96 percent of respondents believed honesty is a value that should be taught in school.

Some of the character education programs are rather modest. Elementary schools may, for example, label a hallway "Responsibility Lane" or design a lesson plan to coincide with a month that may be named "Courtesy Month" or "Caring Month." Meanwhile, high schools have started adopting honor codes, similar to the codes that many college students are asked to sign when they enroll. Typically, a high school honor code would ask a student to pledge:

- not to commit plagiarism;
- not to cheat on tests or homework;
- not to buy term papers from the Internet or other sources;
- not to ask someone else to do their homework;
- not to submit the same project to two different courses; and
- not to sabotage anybody else's school work.

Esther Schaeffer, head of the Washington-based Character Education Project which helps schools establish programs on ethics, told David Callahan, "A school where you've got good character education is one where the culture of the school puts a

Although cheating may lead to success, it often results in serious consequences, as was the situation in the collapse of the energy corporation Enron. In January 2001 Enron was one of the wealthiest U.S. companies, but by December of that year it had filed for bankruptcy. As federal investigations into the company's financial activities turned up evidence of wrongdoing, numerous top executives were charged with malfeasance, including former Enron CEO Kenneth Lay, shown here being escorted in handcuffs into a federal court after being indicted for wire fraud and conspiracy in July 2004. Those who were hurt the most by the cheating of Lay and other executives, were the tens of thousands of unwitting Enron employees and stockholders who trusted Lay when he said the company was sound. Most of them lost their investments when Enron collapsed.

high premium on respect, honesty, and kids being responsible for their actions and adults doing the same."

Still, some educators see teaching ethics as a very difficult task. After all, they argue, schools train students to be competitive—in sports, certainly, but also in academics—so they can be prepared for a competitive society. They point out that teaching ethics means teaching students how to be competitive while still playing fair. "One is about competition and the other is about cooperation," Gordon M. Ambach, executive director of the National Council of Chief State School Officers, told the *New York Times*.

Recent studies have shown the difficulty of effectively teaching ethics to students. A study conducted in 2010 by the Institute of Education Sciences, the U.S. Department of Education's research arm, found that, for the most part, character education programs don't produce any improvements in student behavior or academic performance. The study indicated that the most effective character education programs involved a total schoolwide process, in which ethics were incorporated into all subjects.

Educators do agree that if young people do not get the message about ethics in high school and they do not get it in college, then they are likely to try bending the rules once they join the working world. There is no clearer example of that than the young people who cheat on their résumés, fabricating backgrounds for themselves so they can enhance their chances of getting a job. Typically, they may falsely claim to have received honors or degrees in college, or they may have made up an internship to show they have on-the-job training. Sometimes job applicants get away with fabricating résumés, sometimes, they do not. People who lie on their résumés are often caught by a company's human resources department, which will look into the backgrounds of job applicants. In the case of a recent college graduate seeking employ-ment, a human resources office would typically check with the university to make sure the applicant obtained the degree he or she claims on the résumé, and it will check with the company that sponsored an internship to make sure the applicant worked there. Robert P. Lawry, director of the Center for Professional Ethics at Case Western University in Ohio, told the *New York Times*, "People are thinking, 'It's a competitive world out there, and I'm just going to get lost in the shuffle if I don't put my best foot forward,' even if it's not true. But in the end, you will get lost."

Lying on a résumé is just one more opportunity to cheat. But it is hardly the final opportunity. If young people emerge from a cul-ture in which they have gotten away with cheating on tests, or have plagiarized term papers by using the Internet, or have read a *Cliffs Notes* study guide instead of the whole book, or have used steroids, or illegally downloaded music, upon reaching adulthood they will probably look for other ways to cheat. Perhaps income will be understated on federal tax forms to pay less taxes. Perhaps a way will be discovered to cut into the TV cable without paying a hookup fee or monthly charge. Perhaps they will walk out of a busy restaurant without paying the bill. Perhaps a little cheating here and there will lead to much bigger crimes. As Fred Dellorfano told the Susquehanna University students, "At some point in the future, you may have second thoughts about doing the littlest things that you might feel is maybe not too illegal . . . And that's really where it all starts."

Glossary

ANABOLIC—in medicine, the formation of complex living organisms from simple organisms; an anabolic steroid uses proteins to form muscle mass. Anabolic comes from a Greek word that means "to build up."

BOOKMAKING—illegal enterprise in which the bookmaker, or "bookie," accepts bets on the outcome of sporting events from gamblers.

COPYRIGHT—exclusive right, granted by law, for use of written, artistic, or musical material.

DEFENDANTS—persons accused of wrongdoing in criminal or civil court.

DIAGNOSIS—analysis conducted to identify a disease or similar physical or mental handicap, typically conducted by a physician or other medical professional.

DISCLAIMERS—published notices alerting readers that the person who has written a book or report or produced a movie or TV show takes no responsibility for the accuracy of its content.

DYSLEXIA—learning disability that makes reading difficult.

ENTREPRENEURS—persons who start and run businesses.

ETHICS—rules of moral conduct, typically requiring members of a society to respect the law and the rights of each other.

FELONIES—category of serious crimes, usually punishable by prison sentences.

FINANCIERS—persons who supply money to establish or expand businesses.

INTEGRITY—rigid adherence to a code of values.

INTERNSHIP—paid or unpaid job performed in a company or similar organization by a student seeking on-the-job training; typically, colleges award credits for internships.

LAWSUITS—document filed in civil court accusing a defendant of wrongdoing and usually demanding cash payment.

Glossary

PIRACY—with regard to intellectual property, making use of the copyrighted or patented work of another without permission.

PLAGIARISM—taking the words and ideas of another person and claiming them as one's own.

PORNOGRAPHIC—graphic depictions of sexual activity.

PROBATION—period of supervision in which a person's activities are under close scrutiny; a student serving time on academic probation would face expulsion if he or she violates the school's rules or continues to receive failing grades.

PROCTOR—person appointed to supervise students while they take a test.

RACKETEERING—illegal activity by professional criminals.

RÉSUMÉS—documents written by job applicants to outline their personal, academic, and employment backgrounds.

RIGGED—manipulated dishonestly for personal gain.

ROYALTIES—money paid to authors, musicians, and others who hold copyrights on their work.

SOUNDTRACK—music written to accompany a film.

STEROIDS—drugs that assist a body's ability to manufacture muscle.

VALEDICTORIAN—student who delivers a speech at graduation, usually selected because he or she ranks first academically in the class.

VERBATIM—word for word.

Internet Resources

http://www.gallup.com

Visitors to the site maintained by The Gallup Organization can find results of numerous surveys undertaken by the national polling firm.

http://www.josephsoninstitute.org

The Ethics of American Youth report cards, which are issued every two years, can be accessed at the Web site maintained by the California-based Josephson Institute.

http://www.charactercounts.org

Website of Character Counts!, a national program meant to help young people learn trustworthiness, respect, responsibility, fairness, caring, and citizenship.

http://www.drugabuse.gov/drugs-abuse/steroids-anabolic

Health hazards of using steroids are explored at the National Institute on Drug Abuse site. The page also includes a link to the institute's lengthy report, *Anabolic Steroid Abuse*, which provides extensive information on the scope and consequences of steroid use in America.

http://www.character.org

Visitors to the site of the Washington-based Character Education Partnership can learn about Character Education projects at schools throughout the country.

http://www.riaa.org

Young people thinking about illegally downloading songs from the Internet would do well to first visit the Recording Industry Association of America's site. The organization defines music piracy, explains the penalties for copyright infringement, and provides information on how the RIAA enforces its members' copyrights.

Internet Resources

http://www.turnitin.com/en_us/home

Turnitin is an online company that specializes in checking papers and other written material for plagiarism. The site includes information for students explaining what plagiarism is, and tips on how to avoid it while writing term papers by properly citing sources and developing good research and writing skills.

http://www.academicintegrity.org/icai/home.php

The International Center for Academic Integrity works to promote the values of academic integrity among students, faculty, teachers, and administrators. This website contains information about the center and its activities.

Publisher's Note: The websites listed in this book were active at the time of publication. The publisher is not responsible for websites that have changed their address or discontinued operation since the date of publication. The publisher reviews and updates the websites each time the book is reprinted.

Further Reading

Alderman, John. *Sonic Boom: Napster, MP3, and the New Pioneers of Music.* New York: Perseus Publishing, 2001.

Bazerman, Max H., and Ann E. Tenbrunsel. *Blind Spots: Why We Fail to Do What's Right and What to Do about It.* Princeton, N.J.: Princeton University Press, 2011.

Callahan, David. *The Cheating Culture.* New York: Harcourt, 2004.

Cooper, Chris. *Run, Swim, Throw, Cheat: The Science Behind Drugs in Sports.* New York: Oxford University Press, 2012.

Gilmore, Barry. *Plagiarism: A How-Not-To Guide for Students.* Portsmouth, N.H.: Heinemann, 2009.

Neville, Colin. *The Complete Guide to Referencing and Avoiding Plagiarism.* New York: McGraw-Hill, 2010.

Taylor, William N. *Anabolic Steroids and the Athlete.* Jefferson, N.C.: McFarland and Co., 2002.

Whitley, Bernard E. Jr., and Patricia Keith-Spiegel. *Academic Dishonesty: An Educator's Guide.* Mahwah, N.J.: Lawrence Erlbaum, 2002.

Zimniuch, Fran. *Crooked: A History of Cheating in Sports.* Lanham, Md.: Taylor Trade Publishing, 2009.

Index

Numbers in **bold italic** refer to captions and graphs.

Index

Index

Index

Picture Credits

Contributors

GEORGE GALLUP JR. (1930–2011) was involved with The Gallup Organization for more than 50 years. He served as chairman of The George H. Gallup International Institute and served on many boards involved with health, education, and religion, including the Princeton Religion Research Center, which he co-founded.

Mr. Gallup was internationally recognized for his research and study on youth, health, religion, and urban problems. He wrote numerous books, including *My Kids On Drugs?* with Art Linkletter (Standard, 1981); *The Great American Success Story* with Alec Gallup and William Proctor (Dow Jones-Irwin, 1986); *Growing Up Scared in America* with Wendy Plump (Morehouse, 1995); *Surveying the Religious Landscape: Trends in U.S. Beliefs* with D. Michael Lindsay (Morehouse, 1999); and *The Next American Spirituality* with Timothy Jones (Chariot Victor Publishing, 2002).

Mr. Gallup received his BA degree from the Princeton University Department of Religion in 1954, and held seven honorary degrees. He received many awards, including the Charles E. Wilson Award in 1994, the Judge Issacs Lifetime Achievement Award in 1996, and the Bethune-DuBois Institute Award in 2000. Mr. Gallup passed away in November 2011.

THE GALLUP YOUTH SURVEY was founded in 1977 by Dr. George Gallup to provide ongoing information on the opinions, beliefs and activities of America's high school students and to help society meet its responsibility to youth. The topics examined by the Gallup Youth Survey have covered a wide range—from abortion to zoology. From its founding through the year 2001, the Gallup Youth Survey sent more than 1,200 weekly reports to the Associated Press, to be distributed to newspapers around the nation.

HAL MARCOVITZ is a Pennsylvania-based journalist. He has written more than 50 books for young readers. His other titles for the Gallup Youth Survey series include *Teens and Career Choices* and *Teens and Volunteerism*. He lives in Chalfont, Pennsylvania, with his wife, Gail, and daughters Ashley and Michelle.